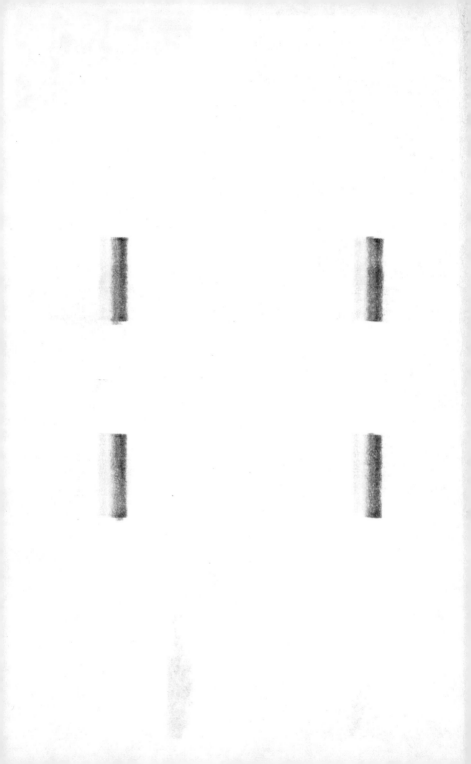

The Hoe and the Horse on the Plains

THE HOE AND

ON

A Study of Cultural Development

PRESTON HOLDER

THE HORSE
THE PLAINS

among North American Indians

University of Nebraska Press Lincoln·London

Publishers on the Plains

UNP

First Bison Book Printing: December 1974

The most recent printing is indicated by the first digit below:
3   4   5   6   7   8   9   10

Manufactured in the United States of America

Contents

A picture section follows page 50.

Introduction

This study concerns two native modes of life on the Great Plains—hoe farming and hunting from horseback—as they fared in the face of Europe's intrusion into the New World. Village gardeners were old residents along the rivers, but equestrian skills, newly acquired from Europeans, allowed bands of expert hunters to spread their nomadic life around the villages and on across the uplands in pursuit of bison herds. Conflicts engendered in that process are a central theme in this essay, stressing the partisan viewpoint of the horticulturalists as they faced the wandering hunters on the one hand and the Europeans on the other. Consideration of the two contrasting patterns of life also shows something of the personal arena in which culture change is initiated. The descendants of those people, with their traditions, much transformed, are a living part of our national heritage. This contribution can be considered a part of their history, so largely unwritten or submerged within the official versions of the foreign visitor who came to stay.

The newcomer was not aware of a great portion of human history standing behind these New World peoples. During some ten thousand years they had discovered and explored an entire hemisphere. They learned to live with its vast range of environments, domesticating new plants and animals and inventing ceramics, weaving, metalwork, and other arts. At times they lived in cities, built great states, created systems of writing, mathematics, and religious ideologies. They achieved this cultural richness on a simple material base. They were at most gardeners living, in terms of Old World prehistory, at an early Neolithic level. Their skills in horticulture and village life had spread northward from Middle America into the arid Southwest, and more extensively throughout the drainage systems of the mid-continent. Still the lives of the gardeners were interlaced with pursuit of wild provender, and their villages were surrounded and interpenetrated by groups who exclusively followed such simple practices. North America was the largest area of the world, aside from Australia, left to hunters when Europeans began their rapid expansion across the continent.

The course of European penetration and consolidation was uneven. The northeast coast and the far Southwest were settled early, but whole sections of the interior long remained unknown. In the seventeenth and eighteenth centuries the Plains were remote. Fur traders explored westward from the Great Lakes and the Mississippi River; a few Spaniards wandered north and east from Mexico; but the details of the country and its people were unknown until the nineteenth century. The map (facing p. 32) shows the location of the more important groups at that time. Along the eastern border are the village dwellers in various phases of changing their way of life. In the far south are the Caddos and their linguistic relatives, the Wichitas and Kitsais. North of them in order are the Siouan-speaking Osages, Kansas, Omahas, and Poncas. On their west are the Caddoan Pawnees, and to the north the related Arikaras with the closely associated Siouan Mandans and Hidatsas. The other groups are equestrian nomads of uncertain location, all in different stages of transition. These people were introduced to the horse and other European elements while in relative isolation. They developed a new way of life, equestrian hunting, and within a few generations the Plains were filled with tribes who diverged widely in language and background. They shared, however, a strikingly uniform material culture, which led the layman and the anthropologist alike to the idea of the Plains Indian. Examination shows that there were important differences among these groups which must be explored.

The examination utilizes archeological, ethnological, and historical materials. History suffices to chart the course of European expansion and it also furnishes insight into the evanescent minutiae of daily life. The fragmentary archeological record helps to sketch in the overall patterns of life in prehistoric times. Ethnology furnishes the most valuable aid, but the information was gathered from a nomadic point of view, so to speak. This study leans toward a village point of view and shows what life was like along the rivers before the horse appeared.

The nature of those records reflects the course of historical development. From the sixteenth through the eighteenth centuries come the incidental observations of adventurers and explorers, military, religious, and commercial. The nineteenth century saw natural scientists amassing information with only occasional interest in the native people. After the mid-century, government agencies concerned themselves with intensive studies of single tribes and also attacked specific ethnological problems. In the opening decades of the twentieth century major museums began systematic studies, not only of tribal groups, but also of special subjects. Studies also came from individuals with only nominal institutional affiliation.

After some decades of this intensive work Clark Wissler's idea of a uniform Plains Culture Area had a considerable following.[1] In essence it was a stereotype based on material culture and some striking ceremonial activity, found mainly among the bison hunters. Edward Sapir and others early recognized that many traits were imported from outside areas, and a late flowering was suspected for the whole pattern.[2] By the 1930s this latter view led to the idea that the Plains could not be considered a stable uniform culture area. Rather the culture was compounded of intrusive ideas, and was a late phenomenon of only seeming stability.

The unique position of the Pawnees and their linguistic relatives had been noted for some time. J. R. Murie's observations, as recorded by S. A. Dorsey, had emphasized their rich religious ideology. Their practice of human sacrifice had caused speculations about Middle American origins. Ruth Benedict, as well as Elsie Clews Parsons, had noted how their religion varied from that thought typical of the Plains. A. Lesser and Gene Weltfish's intensive work in the late 1920s furnished corroboration and indicated that their central position could well be ancient and their ethnological importance out of keeping with their small numbers.[3] Subsequent ethno-

[1] Wissler, 1917, and later editions, gives a popular presentation.
[2] Sapir, 1916, p. 45. Kroeber, 1939, pp. 78–79, also discusses this theory.
[3] S. A. Dorsey, passim; Wissler and Spinden, 1916; Linton, 1926; Benedict, 1922; Parsons, 1929; Lesser, and Weltfish, all titles.

logical studies on the Plains increasingly followed Lesser's concern with acculturation and the distressing life on the reservations.

Another facet was brought into focus through archeological facts. George F. Will had shown early in the century that considerable archeological research could be done in old village sites. In the 1930s W. D. Strong summarized some three decades of such work in the east-central Plains and polemically attacked the validity of Wissler's Plains Culture Area.[4] Stressing a direct historical approach, he traced the villages into prehistoric times and established stability of residence, especially for the Pawnees. It was in this atmosphere, after some experience in the archeology of the Mississippi Valley and the Southeast, that I initiated the present study. Field work with the Arikaras and subsequent library research on related peoples again emphasized the signal importance of the Caddoan peoples and led to the design of this essay.

Following World War II there was a sudden increase in federally sponsored archeological research. The main work lay in the middle reaches of the Missouri Valley. The immediate aim was to retrieve materials threatened by impounded waters of flood-control projects. The work perforce resulted in the testing of debris from many ancient villages along the immediate course of the stream. A wealth of information came from randomly scattered prehistoric intervals and is just now seeing publication.

In this study the central and northern Caddoan peoples are a point of focus. Deriving their way of life anciently from centers along the Mississippi River, their pattern serves as the

[4] Will and Spinden, 1906; Strong, 1933, 1935, 1936. See also Wedel, 1936, 1938.

example for the role of the horticulturalists in native culture change of the eighteenth and nineteenth centuries, other villagers being considered as variants. The Dakota Sioux furnish the example of rising equestrian bison hunters in contrast to the villagers. The whole process must be seen in the light of increasing European contacts. The collapse of village economy and the rise of nomadism are both a result of native adaptations of foreign elements incidentally introduced as part of Europe's economic growth. New utilization of old hunting resources developed, and expansion into untapped environments followed. Ecological factors alone do not explain the process. The conservatism of the villagers and the resilience of the hunters also stemmed from the overall patterning of the way of life, further strengthened by the social ordering and supporting ideologies in which the individual operated. Within the villages there was a settling out of interest which not only fostered traditional stability but also created ferment and tension for some. Among the nomads a more loosely ordered community fitted the new situation and even found adherents within the village ordering. In the final analysis the stability of the villages was a matter of ancient indigenous ideology which came from the nature of village life and in turn supported it.

Most of these ideas were incorporated in an unpublished dissertation at Columbia University in the late 1940s. They have since circulated in microfilm and other forms, appearing in different guises. I have reworked the original materials, added new data, reexamined information in the light of more recent discoveries, enriched the supporting discussion, and sharpened the original argument. I have tried to make this account interesting to the nonspecialist, but have nonetheless endeavored to present it in a fashion useful to the specialist.

The General Setting

Within the United States the Plains area is roughly contained within the boundaries of the bank of states running south from North Dakota to the Gulf Coast region of Texas. On the west the border is marked by the foothills of the Rocky Mountains. Toward the east the Plains fade off into the central lowlands along an irregular north-south line between the 96th and 100th meridians. In its essentials the country is a huge, slightly tilted surface of sedimentary formations with a soil mantle of erosional debris, rising slowly in elevation until in the western stretches the surface is some four thousand to five thousand feet above sea level.

I

There are many patches of rough country within the region: the outfingerings of the dissected uplift that forms the Black Hills; the Badlands of South Dakota; the Pembina and Turtle mountains of North Dakota; the Sandhill region of Nebraska; the Smoky Hills and Flint Hills of Kansas; the Wichita, Cookson, and Arbuckle hills of Oklahoma; and the westward extensions of the Ozark uplift. Nevertheless, the Great Plains are generally considered as a single physiographic unit with an associated typical climate and relatively uniform floral and faunal population.[1]

The north-south orientation of the westerly mountains facilitates the movement of large air masses into the area from the Arctic regions as well as from the Gulf, creating extremes of temperature and wind. Characteristic line squalls or thunderstorms in the summer and blizzards during the winter are a reflection of these factors. The climate is typically continental with extreme annual temperature variations occurring far into the southerly reaches. There is, however, a prevailing easterly direction in the movement of air from the Pacific across the continent. Warm moisture-laden southerly air mingling with cold northerly and westerly air masses accounts for most of the annual precipitation, which averages no more than twenty inches west of the 100th meridian. Where the Plains merge into the central valley lowlands, rainfall increases to as much as thirty-five inches a year.

In spite of the semiarid character of most of the Plains, the moisture caught by the western mountain barrier is sufficient to form a multitude of perennial drainage systems running to the eastward across the tilted surface. These streams have dissected the flat uplands to a relatively low gradient, and lack

[1] Kroeber, 1939, discusses this matter, pp. 76–88.

highly developed meander systems until the great rivers of the eastern borders are reached. From north to south these river systems form a ladderlike arrangement, so that the surface of the Plains in detail is actually a complex of gently rising and falling hills, interrupted at intervals by the stream courses proper. Throughout the whole area the streams have cut down through the uplands to flow along wide alluvium-covered bottoms, often one hundred or more feet below the surrounding plain. The stream course itself with its permanent subsurface water table is bordered with a series of terraces or benches. The lowermost are flooded annually during the spring runoffs. Beyond the terraces at the valley edge steep bluffs rise abruptly to the uplands, often some miles away from the actual stream.

These drainage systems have great bearing on the whole prehistory and history of the Plains. In their rich alluvial bottoms the key to the prehistoric archeological sequence has been found. It was up these same bottoms that the major European penetration of the region came. The European explorers moving westward out of the central valley lowlands were acutely conscious of the ecological shift that marks the Great Plains. They also had a clear understanding of the significance of the streams. The river bottoms, in effect, form a completely different ecological zone from that of the surrounding Great Plains. The river systems with their rich alluvium and constant water supply form wooded extensions of the central valley ecological zone which finger westward far out into the Plains proper. The heavy phytographic cover and its attendant life forms are in sharp contrast to the grass-covered uplands with their typical Plains fauna.

The dichotomy between the two types of tribes occupying the Plains area at the time of exploration has been noted above.

3

The completely nomadic hunting groups with their horse-borne culture occupied the vast upland Plains as a function of their dependence on the bison herds for their supplies of food. The riverine groups, on the other hand, were dependent upon horticultural products for the bulk of their basic food supply. They lived in permanent, if intermittently occupied, villages located along the river courses, and it was to this land that they were tied.

The river courses also served as avenues of access to the Plains area for various populations over hundreds of years before the opening of the historic period, and it was up these channels that the expanding European colonial powers moved, with such drastic effect on the native populations all along the way.

The discovery of the Western Hemisphere was followed by efforts of the European nations to consolidate new positions and push forward into the wealth of the new continents. In North America the first French and English activities were concentrated along the eastern seaboard. The Spaniards, however, in keeping with a hemisphere-wide policy, immediately began the task of exploring the new wilderness. A bare fifty years after the discovery of the New World they were ready to attempt the initial European penetration of the interior.

The Spanish approach came from the south in two prongs. One, aimed westward toward the middle region of the Mississippi River, was the expedition under the command of Hernando De Soto. By 1542 De Soto's party reached the country that is now western Arkansas and eastern Texas. The hostility which they had already met at the hands of the native inhabitants was here duplicated with such violence that they were forced to fall back on the Mississippi and continue a retreat to the south. Their stay, brief as it was, gives us some pertinent comments on the cultures of the region.

The other prong of the attack fared little better. This was the expedition under the command of Francisco Vásquez de Coronado which in 1541 pushed across the Plains northeast of the Spanish holdings in New Mexico. Somewhere near central Kansas, in Quivira, they came into contact with riverine horticultural groups, evidently the people now known as the Wichitas.[2]

Some fifty years later an unauthorized Spanish expedition, that of Francisco Leya de Bonilla and Antonio Gutierrez de Humaña, again found the grass-lodge villages of horticultural peoples along the middle reaches of the Arkansas River. Their expedition was followed in 1599 by Vicente de Zaldivar's exploration to the north and east from New Mexico. Two years later Juan de Oñate led an expedition into the territory which had been explored by Humaña. The accounts of these trips clearly differentiate foot nomads, who lived by following the bison herds, from the people with whom they maintained a sort of symbiotic relationship, the horticultural Pueblo villages on the west and the riverine peoples east and northeast, including the peoples of Quivira. Spanish efforts were spread over a vast territory and interest in the exploration of Quivira seems to have lapsed for some time after these initial incidents.[3]

The French, English, and Dutch concentrated their efforts along waterways leading into the continent from the northeast.

---

[2] Swanton, 1942, pp. 29–35 ff., gives details of these expeditions as well as later efforts. Hammond and Ray, 1940, and Wedel, 1961, pp. 102 ff., should also be consulted.

[3] Hammond and Ray, 1940, p. 261, discuss trade relations. Bolton, 1916, pp. 200–67, gives details of the expeditions.

During the first quarter of the seventeenth century the French under Samuel de Champlain followed the St. Lawrence and its affluents into the Great Lakes as far west as the Georgian Bay country of present western Ontario. In the 1630s Jean Nicolet reached the Wisconsin territory around Green Bay, but the records of his trip are vague and confused. The ultimate result of these European activities was a general movement of Iroquois groups raiding far to the westward.

By 1653 Iroquois raiders were harassing native groups around Green Bay, and in 1665 they attacked the Illinois in the Wisconsin country. This period is rife with intermittent warfare related to the activities of the European colonial powers in their eastern holdings. Again in 1669 the Iroquois were moving against the Foxes in the Wisconsin country. Such native military adventures were accompanied by the displacement of many groups. The Hurons and Ottawas were wandering far to the west of their homeland around 1660 when they introduced European trade goods to the Sioux. The native inhabitants on the fringe of the whole Great Lakes basin were pushed westward into the Wisconsin and Illinois country during the middle of the seventeenth century.

This movement westward appears to have been followed in the 1670s by a gradual resurgence of the displaced peoples back to the east as the Iroquois power waned. Nevertheless, the Iroquois were still fighting deep in the Illinois country in 1677, 1680, and 1684. The period from 1650 to 1750 seems to have been crucial in initiating the southwesterly movements which ultimately erupted the Dakota Sioux across the Missouri River barrier of horticultural villages and thence out onto the Plains.[4]

[4] General comments and specific details can be found in Blair, 1911, and Hunt, 1940.

It is clear from the French records that the cultural changes occurring on this continent were not simply a matter of the activities of the Europeans and their influence on the native groups. The influences were mutual. The native groups reacted to European innovations in ways that inevitably changed their cultures and the Europeans modified themselves in the face of native cultures. This is nowhere better illustrated than in the solution which the French found to the problems they faced in their initial commercial penetration of the interior of the continent. They evidently realized that the European cultural pattern was inadequate for the problems posed by an unfamiliar environment until a more extensive facsimile of European conditions had been imported and adjusted to the new surroundings.

Their solution was a simple one, and one followed many years later by the commercial representatives of the United States in tapping the fur resources of the western mountain areas: namely, that of accepting and adopting native methods and of becoming dependent on the native groups for survival. The French developed a system which utilized lower-class members who had much to gain and little to lose in changing cultures. Working as individuals, these men formed the avant-garde of French colonial ambitions. Taking the native peoples as their model and becoming somewhat more than half native themselves, they sketched in the lines of communication and supply which were later expanded in an organized fashion. In addition, they established the framework of commercial procedure by means of which native labor could be successfully utilized in working the wealth of the interior fur resources.

In changing cultures these men may well have found more status among the indigenous people than they had in their own society. Nevertheless, occasional ones were rewarded with high

7

status, like François-Marie Perrot, who began as a lowly
engagé for the Jesuits and over the years became an influential
explorer deeply involved in government plans. The later
example of Etienne Véniard de Bourgmont will be seen below.
He began as a *voyageur*, founded families in Indian communities, explored the Missouri River country, and then
became an influential respected member of the community
directing the fur trade. Whatever their personal motivation,
these men ultimately constituted a genuine profession of
skilled workmen organized into a complex hierarchy of
voyageurs, *coureurs de bois*, *hivernants*, and *mangeurs de lard*,
under the direction of the *commis* or *bourgeois*. Everywhere in
the spheres of French operations they formed the forefront of
contact with the indigenous groups.[5]

Unfortunately, few of these men were literate, and there is
little adequate record of the wealth of knowledge which the
voyageurs must have possessed regarding the native cultures.
Thus it must always be borne in mind that official records of
French contacts with native groups often followed initial
contacts by many years

There is a rather indefinite period of time stretching from the
first actual European intercourse with the native groups to the
time of adequate historical documentation. With considerable
insight into this problem Plains archeologists frequently
separate the conventional categories of "historic" and "prehistoric" by an intervening period, the "protohistoric." In the
area of French influence on the Plains the protohistoric period

[5] There seems to be no single work summarizing and supporting
these general and specific statements. Useful but scattered are:
Margry, 1876–88, vols. 1 and 6; Masson, 1889–90; Lahontan, 1905;
Kellogg, 1917, 1925; Kenton, 1927; Nute, 1931, 1943; Giraud,
1945, 1953, 1958a, 1958b.

is thus characterized by a long span of direct and intensive native contact with *voyageurs* living among them. The intermittent contact from the east continued with increasing frequency as the trade reached farther up the westerly affluents of the Mississippi, the visitors spending longer times in the native settlements. The native groups reflected the restlessness and increasingly felt the impact of the new goods and ideas that came as a consequence.

By the end of the seventeenth century the French had shifted their official focus of interest to include the Mississippi Valley. French expansion down the Mississippi River was formally initiated by Louis Jolliet's trip in 1675. His party reached the neighborhood of the mouth of the Arkansas River before returning upstream. Although several of the horticultural tribes of the eastern edge of the Plains are mentioned on maps, presumably from data gathered by this party, no descriptions have been found. The records associated with the La Salle expeditions of 1682 and 1687 offer the earliest French characterization of the horticulturalists in the southeastern portion of our area of interest.

In the years 1695, 1697, 1700, and 1702, "Navajos" and "Apaches" raiding far eastward from the southwestern Spanish settlements reported meeting isolated Europeans visiting in the villages of Plains horticultural groups, apparently the Pawnees or Wichitas. In 1703, 20 *voyageurs* left from the Mississippi to "discover New Mexico." In 1704, 110 *voyageurs* were reported along the Mississippi and Missouri rivers scattered in small bands of 8 or 10 men.

In 1705 "*un nommé Laurain,*" having been up the Missouri River, there met native groups who had knowledge of the Spaniards, and in 1706 two *Canadiens* had spent two years

9

moving from village to village along the Missouri. Juan de Ulibarri's Spanish expedition to El Cuartelejo near Wichita or Pawnee territory in 1706 met "Apaches" who had attacked a horticultural village to the east where they killed and scalped a European. Among their loot was a "red-lined cap," a traditional element of the *voyageur*'s costume. In 1708 "*voyageurs canadiens*" were reported to have ascended the Missouri River some three hundred to four hundred leagues. Marcel Giraud, on the basis of a reexamination of some basic documents, claims that Bourgmont visited the country of the Arikaras as early as 1714. Pedro Villasur's expedition from New Mexico in 1720 met French nationals among the Pawnees far to the west. In 1723 a *voyageur*, LaFleur, who had been with the Mahas (Omahas) reported them in alliance with the Ricaras (Arikaras) some ten leagues from the village which he visited. "*Un Francois*," having lived with the Panimahas (Skiri Pawnees) for some years before 1734, had gone with them to visit the Arikaras, who, he said, had never before seen a Frenchman. Two *voyageurs* who accompanied him verified his report. The discrepancy between this statement and Bourgmont's claims remains to be resolved. It may well be that we are dealing with different and widely separated Arikara villages.[6]

The French continued their expansion to the west of the Mississippi River throughout the first half of the eighteenth century. In the south Jean-Baptiste le Moyne de Bienville reached Caddo villages on the Red River by 1700. After repeated visits to the Caddos in the intervening years, Louis Jouchereau de St. Denis made an extended journey to Mexico

[6] Thomas, 1935, pp. 13–14, 67, 133–37, 226, 234. Margry, 1876–88, vol. 6, pp. 160, 180–83, 385, 455. Giraud, 1953, pp. 330–33; 1958a, p. 195; 1958b.

through their country in 1714–16 at the request of Spanish missionaries. Bernard de la Harpe's expedition of 1719 established a post among the Nasoni group of the Caddos and explored westward up the Red River, ultimately coming into contact with Wichita groups near the confluence of the Arkansas and Canadian rivers, where he learned of the Pawnees and Arikaras far to the north. In the same year Charles Claude du Tisné pushed westward from the Mississippi to the Osage villages and traveled southwesterly across streams draining into the "*riviere des osages*" and reached the "Panys" (Wichitas ?). Farther north the pattern of official French penetration of the Plains was extended during the years 1722–24 when Bourgmont founded Fort Orleans on the lower Missouri River and explored to the southwest, passing through Kansa territory and ultimately meeting groups of Padoucas.

By 1739 the penetration of the Plains had gone so far that trading expeditions were successful in reaching Santa Fe. In that year the Mallet brothers ascended the Missouri and its affluents to the Skiri Pawnee settlements. Previous exploratory efforts had tried to locate a passage to New Mexico by way of the headwaters of the Missouri River, and, as noted, the French had ascended this river as far as the Arikara villages some time before. The Pawnees advised the Mallets to take a different route following the Platte River and its affluents. They reached Santa Fe, guided part of the way by an Arikara slave whom they found at a "Laitane" (Comanche) village, and returned to the French bases later by way of the Red or the Arkansas River.[7]

[7] Swanton, 1942, pp. 50–59. Margry, 1876–88, vol. 6, pp. 293, 309–15, 385–452, 456–92, includes Fabry de la Bruyère's attempt to follow the Mallet route. Mooney, 1896, p. 1043, and Hodge, 1912, pp. 1064, 1081, indicate the Comanche identification.

At about this same time the French were active along the upper reaches of the Missouri River, moving out from establishments in the lake country of the north. Acting under specific orders from Beauharnois to find a route to the western sea, Pierre Gaultier de Varennes, Sieur de La Vérendrye and his sons tried in 1738 and again in 1742–43 to discover a western pass by way of the villages of the Mandans on the upper Missouri. Although in their last attempt they reached the foothills of the Rocky Mountains, the ethnographic details found in their documents leave much to be desired.[8]

In the central portion of the Plains the route to the Platte River and the Skiri Pawnee villages was followed again in 1752 by a trading venture more ambitious than that of the Mallets. In that year Jean Chapuis and Louis Feulli made the passage from the Illinois country to the lower Platte River, thence to the Kansa villages and on across the Plains to New Mexico. They took with them an astonishing amount of trade goods for both the native and the Spanish markets. From their statements to the Santa Fe authorities it is evident that they planned to set up a caravan route from Illinois to New Mexico. They hoped to trade with the intervening people, buying horses from the "Pawnees" and Comanches in order to transport their goods from the head of navigation on across the Plains.[9]

Similar French parties were active in the southern stretches of the Plains at this time. In 1748 the Comanches brought word to Taos that thirty-three Frenchmen had visited their villages and traded muskets to them. In the next year three deserters from the French establishment at Arkansas Post near

[8] Margry, 1876–88, vol. 6, pp. 590–92, 598–611; La Vérendrye, 1927, pp. 335 ff.

[9] Thomas, 1940, pp. 82–110.

the confluence of the White and Arkansas rivers arrived in Taos after following the Arkansas River to the "Panipiquet or Jumano" (Wichita?) villages, and then through Comanche territory to New Mexico. That autumn a Spaniard named Sandoval started for New Mexico with six companions after having spent some five years with the French in Louisiana. The party ascended the Arkansas River to the two fortified grass-hut villages of the "Jumano" Indians, apparently the very same villages visited by the deserters the previous year. Here they spent twenty days before going on to the Comanches. After a four-month stay with the Comanches they made their way safely to New Mexico, arriving in 1750.[10]

After the initial sixteenth-century explorations Spain followed a pattern of slow and somewhat sporadic expansion out of New Mexico to the east and north. As early as 1650 Franciscan friars seem to have reached native groups on the Trinity River. Toward the end of the century several expeditions under Père Damian Massanet and Alonso de Leon pushed far to the east into the country inhabited by the Caddos proper, where they found ample evidence of La Salle's activities. In 1690 these parties encountered French nationals among the Indians and demonstrated that there was a very real threat of French expansion into territory that was considered to be Spanish. However, by 1711 the Spaniards had reached the point of asking a French national, St. Denis, to assist them in their efforts. Their labors bore fruit in 1716 with the reestablishment of missions among the Caddos proper. In 1719 Governor Martin de Alarçon led an expedition into the area and inspected the missions. Two years later Aguayo visited the area along the Trinity River and in that year the mission of Los

[10] Bolton, 1914, p. 47; 1917, pp. 58–59. Thomas, 1940, pp. 19–20.

Adaes was reestablished to become the capital of the province of Texas. Three new missions had been established in the Texas country by 1731, and in 1754 Governor Jacinto de Barrios y Juarequi demanded the withdrawal of the French from Texas.[11]

Meanwhile the Spaniards were conscious of the French intrusions along the central Plains northeast of New Mexico. The late seventeenth-century reports of French activity in that area were bolstered by the findings of the Ulibarri expedition of 1706 along the headwaters of the Arkansas River. In 1719 on his campaign against the Comanches, Francisco de Valverde y Mercado heard again of French among the "Pawnees and Jumanos" on the central Plains. The threat of these French incursions led to the organization of the expedition under Villasur which may have reached the Platte River in 1720, only to be wiped out by the "Pawnees," with whom there were indeed French associates. Again in 1744 the Spaniards report that a former French soldier, Velo, made his way from the Illinois country across the Plains to Santa Fe.[12]

The European military adventures of the colonial powers in the Seven Years' War brought changes in territorial holdings along the Mississippi River. To the north France ceded all of Canada to England in 1760, and later, in the Treaty of Paris (1763), England received all of the country east of the Mississippi River, with the exception of New Orleans and a few small islands. Spain granted the English rights to Florida but

[11] Bolton, 1916, pp. 345–423; Swanton, 1942, pp. 41–43, 46–48, 51–54.

[12] Thomas, 1935, gives the Valverde and Villasur diaries. La Vérendrye, 1927, p. 416, mentions the Villasur fiasco, which he heard about from natives along the Missouri River far to the north. Velo is in Twitchell, 1914, vol. 2, p. 214.

at the same time received from France the control of Louisiana Territory west of the Mississippi River. The main water route from Quebec to New Orleans was now broken and the old colonial rivalries in the northeast died down.

In the Southwest, Spain immediately moved to consolidate her position in Texas and along the west bank of the lower Mississippi River. The Spanish authorities followed a general policy of utilizing former French personnel and administrative organization. Thus although Padré Gaspar José de Solis of the College of Zacatecas has left a diary of his visits to the Texas missions after the cession in 1767–68, by far the most complete ethnographic data come from the abundant observations of the former French subject Athanase de Mézières during his term of service as lieutenant governor at Natchitoches Post under the Spaniards from 1769 to 1779. These records give many details regarding the effect of the new situation on the native peoples. The southern Caddos proper were by now seriously reduced. Some Skiri Pawnees moved south in the 1770s to take up residence near the still powerful Wichitas. The Osages, their trade contacts with the Illinois country interrupted, emerged as a constant military threat to the peoples on their west. Native military moves were undoubtedly furthered by groups of French and Spanish renegades living in the wilderness along the Arkansas River. It seems likely that the English, who were in direct contact with the Osages by 1777, were using them against the Spaniards. This is one of the basic reasons given by de Mézières for his plan of a military campaign against the Osages in 1777.[13]

[13] Bolton, 1914, vol. 1, pp. 166–67, 202, 284, 301, 304, 306, 330; vol. 2, pp. 90, 122, 136, 141–42, 210–11, 262, 273, 318. Solis, 1931.

The Spaniards were interested in strengthening their position along the Red River in the south. They also recognized the strategic value of the Arkansas and Missouri river drainage systems. In keeping with the new situation they set up a fort, later to become the town of Saint Louis, near the confluence of the Missouri and Mississippi rivers. They began to consolidate their position through a systematic penetration of the country drained by the Missouri as well as of the Arkansas River territory. By 1786 they could report as many as two hundred trappers and traders settled on the upper waters of the latter river. The Spanish penetration appears to have represented a continuation of the French commercial system. In the north the emphasis was still on wresting the fur resources away from the encroaching English. The former French workers were now employed and supervised by organized trading expeditions sent up the Missouri River as far as practicable with orders to build forts to face the English. With the English and Spanish recognition of the threats posed by the other the upper Missouri became an area of increasing interest to both after about 1785.[14]

For the riverine horticulturalists of the middle stretches of the Missouri River the first half of the eighteenth century was filled with intermittent contacts with small parties and single visitors from the European trade. A few trade items from this protohistoric period begin to show up in the debris found by archeologists about the ancient villages. During those years the villagers themselves must have adapted their extensive native trade relations to the new situation and become middlemen. In an expanding wave these native middlemen carried European

[14] Houck, 1909, vol. 1, pp. 1–19, 256. Nasatir, 1929, pp. 362; 1952. Bolton, 1914, vol. 2, pp. 141, 235. Tabeau, 1939, p. 7 n 13.

goods and ideas to the more remote groups, sowing the seeds of serious native rivalries, although their maturing took some time.

Thus the northern villagers were exposed to extensive first-hand contact with the intruding Europeans in the closing quarter of the eighteenth century. A chronological review of some of the major expeditions sent to the upper Missouri River in the closing decades of the eighteenth century and the opening years of the nineteenth century suggests the tempo of the radical change in the cultural setting of the times. In 1787 Joseph Garreau went from Saint Louis to the upper Missouri River, and James MacKay was sent to the Mandan villages. Two years later Munier went to the Poncas on the Niobrara River. In 1790 Jacques d'Eglise briefly visited the upper Missouri country and reached the Mandans. Three years later he returned with Garreau, this time to the Arikara and the Dakota Sioux settlements, while at the same time English traders from Canada were reported at the Mandan villages. In 1794 Jean Baptiste Trudeau (or Truteau), sent from Saint Louis with orders to build a fort near the Mandans, wintered with the Arikaras. Concurrently Réné Jussaume, Juan Fotman (Tremont), and Chrysostome Joncquard came from Canada to the Mandan and Pawnee Hoca (Arikara?) villages. The following year saw several expeditions from Saint Louis: Lecuyer traveled with Pierre Antoine Tabeau to the upper Missouri country, and MacKay and John Evans proceeded independently to the same destination. At the same time North West Company traders came to the Mandans from Canadian bases, as they did again the next year, to be followed by David Thompson's expedition of 1797 to the same villagers. In 1800 Hugh Heney went up the Missouri from Saint Louis, and Régis Loisel probably left from the same base for the upper

Missouri. By 1802 Loisel, from Saint Louis, was at the mouth of the Bad River with orders to build Fort au Cèdres near the Dakota Sioux. In that year François Marie Perrin du Lac as well as Trudeau came upriver to the mouth of the White River. The next year Loisel revisited Fort au Cèdres. In 1804 Tabeau traveled from Saint Louis for a considerable stay with the Arikaras, and Charles McKenzie with François Antoine Larocque reached the Mandans from Canada. This was the general situation at the time the first representatives of the United States, Meriwether Lewis and William Clark, saw the Missouri River country in 1804.[15]

From the ethnographic details given in the records of these expeditions it is clear that the horticultural villages were the major bases of operations for both the English and the Spaniards. Already, however, the equestrian nomadic Dakota Sioux had pushed southeast out of the lake country and were contesting the terrain along the Missouri River between the Arikara settlements and the Omaha-Ponca villages. The trips of the traders upstream were frequently interrupted by the Dakotas. The horticultural peoples were in conflict among themselves over the avenues of trade. These native conflicts were utilized wherever possible by the colonial powers to further their national interests. The traders found that wintering in the horticultural villages was to their advantage, not only for trade, but also to win the allegiance of groups who were in a position to bargain with both the Spaniards and the English. The records of their long winter visits have supplied some of our best ethnographic data for this period.

[15] Documentation for these items will be found passim, but in general order: Nasatir, 1927, pp. 63–69; 1929–30, pp. 365–67, 380, 527; 1952, p. 94. Tabeau, 1939, pp. 9, 39, 26–28. Thompson, 1962, pp. 160–78. Perrin du Lac, 1807. Masson, 1889–90, pp. 299–393.

Meanwhile, in Europe there were further military struggles, as a result of which the United States gained territory west of the Mississippi. In 1800 Spain secretly returned her part of the Louisiana Territory to the French. By April of 1803 the purchase of that territory from France by the United States had been negotiated, and in November, 1803, Louisiana was formally transferred to France, the United States taking possession the following month.

The early expeditions of the United States were primarily interested in exploring the terrain and estimating the inherent wealth of the country. After the first exploratory expedition of Lewis and Clark, with its abundant records, our next source of official information is military, the expedition under Zebulon Montgomery Pike in 1806–1807. A government expedition of thorough scientific intent did not appear until the year 1820, under the command of Stephen H. Long. In the interval between these two official expeditions there are records from the commercial representatives of the American Fur Company and others who went up the Missouri.

Other journals which contain intimate ethnographic details were written somewhat later in the century at a time when the native culture of the sedentary peoples was well on its way out. Nevertheless, we can get some insight into the life of those peoples from the journals kept by such men as James Pattie, Thomas Nuttal, John Bradbury, Henry Brackenridge, John Treat Irving, Charles A. Murray, Victor Tixier, Prince Maximilian, Rudolph Kurz, Henry A. Boller and others who visited or passed through the areas held by the sedentary peoples.

In the records from the turn of the nineteenth century the observers, whether military men or not, were consistently impressed with the amount of native warfare and hostility which they found throughout the area. Not only was there hostility toward the encroaching Europeans, but also native conflicts. The early observers did not exaggerate. The native warfare of the eighteenth and nineteenth centuries ran the gamut from economic blockades and warfare of attrition to guerrilla sniping and pitched battles. Some of the basic motives were economic in nature. But it was merely one manifestation of a thoroughgoing social change which was taking place among the native peoples of the Plains. An old way of life was on its way out and a new way of life was becoming ascendant.

These two ways of life represented fundamentally different accommodations to the environment of the Plains, deriving from distinctive technological traditions with their related socio-economic structures. A new adaptation made possible the utilization of the bison herds on a scale previously impossible. The introduction of equestrian skills permitted an expansion of simple hunting societies to the point where they became, in their new form, the dominant culture of the area. The other adaptation was the horticultural tradition with its roots deep in the prehistory of the Mississippi Valley. These two patterns were in conflict in the face of the advancing European interests, and out of that conflict culture change was emerging. To understand the nature of the changes it is essential to examine in idealized form the basic patterns and the sources of the conflict.

The Village Way of Life

In native North America stable villages of horticulturalists were a relatively late phenomenon. Here as elsewhere in the world they were the result of some thousands of years of cultural development from simple bands of roving hunters and gatherers. Throughout the Mississippi Valley as well as in the American Southwest there is now clear archeological evidence of such a development.[1] In all cases the shift in the pattern of

[1] There is a voluminous literature dealing with the details of this process. It includes not only archeological titles mentioned above, but also a host of obscure papers scattered through many publications. Substantiation for all specific statements will not be attempted, since detailed summaries can be readily found in Wedel, 1961, and Willey, 1966.

settlement seems to be a reflection of the development of horti-cultural practices. Once this development appeared along the Mississippi Valley a new adaptation to the Plains was possible. Horticulturalists were not long in moving out into the river bottoms of the eastern peripheries of the Plains.

Archeological remains of horticulturalists represent at least three different periods in the prehistory of the central Plains, the first of which falls some fifteen hundred or more years ago. There are scattered signs that at that time the Woodland and Hopewell developments of the Mississippi Valley extended well into the central Plains. The Sterns Creek manifestation of the eastern Plains is placed nearly five hundred years later. This intermittently occupied site yields remains of squash seeds. Horticultural evidence from the other complexes is very scanty and it seems probable that cultivation played a small part in the day-to-day existence. Neither is there clear evidence of a settled way of life with villages and stored surpluses. Rather the people seem at best marginal horticulturalists or in many cases hunters and gatherers except for the incidental use of semidomesticated or a very few cultivated plants. The precise details of these early complexes remain to be worked out, but certainly the settlements were not the stable villages of later times, nor have they been demonstrated to have developed locally into any later complexes.

The next period of horticultural occupation exhibits no clear continuity in material culture with the earlier cultures. Now the river bottoms of the central Plains are occupied by scattered settlements which have yielded the remains known under the names of Upper Republican and Nebraska cultures, mani-festations for which the more inclusive terms Aksarben Aspect or, alternatively, Central Plains Aspect, or Tradition, have

24

been suggested. The antecedents of this whole complex are as yet dim. It is not clear whether the cultures represent indigenous and essentially local developments or whether they derived from influences originating in areas outside the Plains proper. The archeological remains seem to cluster in a period roughly some six hundred to one thousand years ago. They are clearly associated with peoples practicing fairly advanced horticulture.

These settlements consist of small clusters of houses scattered along the river terraces or on ridges and bluffs at irregular intervals following a stream course. Since the people cultivated crops it is assumed that their fields lay in the nearby alluvial bottoms. The house clusters can be interpreted as the separate dwellings of extended families working the nearby bottoms cooperatively and sharing the produce.

There are striking analogies with this settlement pattern among the Caddos proper of eastern Texas in the late seventeenth century. Here the French explorers speak of little hamlets of seven or eight or as many as twelve to fifteen houses scattered along the stream courses, often separated by more than a league of empty country. The houses were some sixty feet in diameter and each was occupied by eight or ten families. The hamlets were located wherever the soil was good for cultivation, and the nearby fields were worked cooperatively by the members of the households. Ceremonial centers with larger chief's houses were placed at irregular intervals.[2] They may be analogous to the larger houses occasionally found in Upper Republican archeological sites with infrequent "caches" of what appear to be collections of ceremonial artifacts. If they prove to be the ancestral prototype for the later northern

[2] Margry, 1876–88, vol. 3, pp. 341, 344–45, 387, 393.

Caddoan village bundle, a brief may be made for the organization of these Upper Republican hamlets around some sort of simple ceremonial center. Thus the Upper Republican settlements may also someday prove to contain the seeds of a sociopolitical organization analogous to that of the Caddos proper and to foreshadow the later religio-political developments which will be presented below.

Most Plains archeologists feel that these scattered prehistoric remains are culturally related to the later Caddoan-speaking enclaves of the area. Archeological proof for such a theory is extremely sketchy. Furthermore, in central Nebraska, at least, the sites are generally mantled with a considerable deposit of wind-blown soils, which is taken to indicate a period of abandonment, probably as a result of severe drouth. Thus there is no unequivocal direct line of local cultural continuity leading to the subsequent archeological complex, the proto-historic Lower Loup villages.

However, to the north along the middle stretches of the Missouri River in South Dakota archeological explorations suggest that here may be found a local development from this generalized tradition into later manifestations which seem clearly to be related to historic Caddoan-speaking groups. At the same time it is recognized that these manifestations may be intrusions into a series of settlements already established in the Missouri River country for several centuries. While it is far from convincing, there is some evidence of armed conflict, mainly in the form of so-called defensive earthworks. Regardless of the precise nature of the contacts, there was, after about the sixteenth century, a slow movement of the presumed indigenous groups toward the north. The remaining southerly settlements show increased change and presumed amalgamation leading to the development of a new house type. Certainly by the eighteenth century large, stable villages appeared, a transition which was also occurring among the more northerly groups.

The transition was essentially one leading from small, scattered clusters of farmsteads to large, compact, often fortified villages in late prehistoric and protohistoric times throughout the area. Although direct archeological proof is as yet lacking, many of these villages, probably built in the seventeenth and eighteenth centuries, are considered likely to be immediately ancestral to the Arikara groups of the nineteenth-century accounts. At the same time it is conjectured that to the north the large rectangular (later circular) houses, gathered into orderly arrangements in impressively large villages, were the dwellings of groups ancestral to at least some of the sedentary Siouan-speaking peoples of later times, notably the ethnic entity known as the Mandans. By this reasoning a southward shift of some groups would account for the protohistoric Lower Loup villages of Nebraska. Almost certainly these latter remains are directly ancestral to historic Pawnee groups.[3]

By protohistoric times, along the Missouri River as well as in central Nebraska the settlement pattern had undergone a qualitative change. The villages appear as large, planned communities with considerable population concentrations. Often they are rather elaborately fortified. Instead of lodge clusters scattered along the river bottoms, real, permanent, and stable villages covering many acres had come into being throughout

[3] Lehmer and Caldwell, 1966, offer a summary couched in some of its theoretical implications. Wood, 1967, reviews in detail pertinent Mandan material and offers a different interpretation of some of the same data.

27

the area. The temporal position of this manifestation as well as the occasional appearance of scarce European trade goods in the debris from the sites make it seem likely that some of the growth may be attributed to influences stemming ultimately from European sources. Along with this, as we will see, there was increasing pressure from outside native groups. The acquisition of the horse must have increased the hunting range and the food potential of the villagers as well as extending the range of trade contacts.

Archeological detail regarding the rise of the Wichita groups of Caddoan-speaking peoples is less complete. The historic location of the Wichitas along the Red River is recent. Originally they occupied stable horticultural villages along the bottoms of the Arkansas River drainage system in eastern and central Kansas. Wedel identifies their sixteenth-century location as that of the Quivira of Coronado, and furthermore demonstrates that the protohistoric archeological complexes of the Great Bend Aspect are directly ancestral to these Wichita groups. If we infer from historic practice we may assume that there were frequent contacts between these protohistoric groups and the peoples occupying the Lower Loup sites to the north. There is ample evidence of an earlier occupation of the area by peoples leaving remains falling within the general category of Upper Republican (Central Plains Tradition, Smoky Hill Aspect). Here again there is little sign of a local development into later manifestations and some reason to postulate an abandonment of the area following the Upper Republican occupation. However, large permanent villages appeared and continued throughout late prehistoric and protohistoric times.[4]

[4] Wedel, 1959, pp. 210–379 and especially 625–33.

Archeological research will continue to illuminate the nature of the outside contacts. Certainly we can expect to find that some groups adopted the horse and moved onto the Plains to follow the newly developing pattern of thoroughgoing equestrian nomadism. Much earlier, along the Missouri River actual migrant groups of villagers may have come far west from the great mound centers of the central Mississippi Valley at random intervals during late prehistoric times. Native cultural development there had reached its highest peak at about that time. What influence such migrants may have had on the cultures of the central Plains remains to be seen. Certainly the religious ideology and the social structure of the horticulturalists of the historic period are reminiscent of this order of development. The major orientation in the ideology of the Caddoan-speaking groups, at least, seems to point southward, toward the Caddos proper. There is ample reason to believe that there were also influences felt directly from the east.

In the central Plains it remains to be determined whether the change in the pattern of settlement was slow and gradual or came abruptly. Once the new pattern was formed it never disappeared. Shifts in the size and composition of the specific villages never brought a return to the diffuse pattern of earlier times. In general there seems to have been a tendency among all of the northern Caddoan peoples toward consolidation of villages. The historic descriptions of the villages of the riverine horticulturalists depict a large cluster of relatively permanent habitations to which the people returned year after year, considering them to be the real center of their lives. At the historic level the riverine horticulturalists were gathered into discrete villages along the major stream courses of the eastern Plains. These villages controlled in addition specific wide stretches of the uplands as hunting territories over which the great communal hunts wandered year after year.

The following table of aboriginal population estimates is presented to show the relative population concentrations of the more important Plains horticulturalists. It should assist in differentiating the linguistic relationships of the groups and give some idea of the size of "tribal" divisions, although the figures are rough approximations based on inadequate records.[5]

CADDOAN		SIOUAN	
Arikara	3,000	Mandan-Hidatsa	6,100
Pawnee	10,000	Omaha-Ponca	3,600
Caddo, Wichita, and		Kansa	3,000
other southern		Osage	6,200
Caddoans	13,400		
Total	26,400	Total	18,900

Many of these population figures were greater in prehistoric times. It would appear that as late as the eighteenth century the Arikara figure should be multiplied by at least ten, and the same would seem to hold for the Pawnees. Whether the sedentary Siouan populations were also larger in early times is not so clear. The Mandans, at least, suffered great reduction during the late eighteenth and early nineteenth centuries. The general impression from archeological remains is that ancestral Arikara populations were widespread and dominant along the middle reaches of the Missouri River in late prehistoric and proto-historic times, and the same can be said for the Pawnees, Wichitas, and Caddos to the south. Nevertheless, by historic

[5] Figures from Kroeber, 1939, modifying Mooney's original estimates.

times the total population of the Siouan and the Caddoan sedentary groups was about the same.

A word of caution is in order with regard to the linguistic classification given here. Americanists have long used linguistic affiliation as a handy means of classifying the various "tribal" groups. There is a convenience to such a fundamental classification, since it reveals historical connections between the affiliated members of the group. We are today in some cases able to postulate the relative antiquity of these connections. However, anthropologists early learned that cultural affiliations may run a separate course. Peoples of the same language group may or may not share cultural affiliations; the same can be said for peoples of completely separate language groups. Individuals and indeed groups can radically change their linguistic affiliation over a relatively short time. In the absence of written records such changes are rapidly lost sight of, especially if the peoples involved do not have our overweening interest in linguistic affiliation as a national rallying point. Each case must be examined in its own right.

All of the peoples whom we will discuss in this study, aside from the Algonquian-speaking Cheyennes, belong to one of two great language families: the Caddoan and the Siouan. There is no doubt that the contrast, Caddoan-Siouan, is fundamental and ancient. Of the two groups the Siouan was by far the more widespread and culturally heterogeneous. The Catawbas of the Carolinas as well as the Tutelos and Biloxis of the Gulf Coast are members of this stock. In our area of interest the Siouan-speaking peoples exhibited considerable cultural variation. The Quapaws in the south and the Winnebagos in the north were affiliated culturally with the peoples of the central Mississippi Valley and the Western Great Lakes, respectively. To the west and north the Crows and the Assiniboins are typical Plains tribes, while the Dakotas will serve as our example of equestrian nomads par excellence. The other listed members of this stock are typical village horticulturalists. Many of their attributes are extremely reminiscent of those of the Caddoan-speaking groups, and a classification on the basis of socio-economic adaptations would include them with the Caddoan-speaking village peoples. The small Mandan-Hidatsa group is located far to the north along the Missouri River. While Hidatsa speech is close to Crow, the Mandans are said to have their linguistic ties to the east.

The remaining sedentary Siouans, with the Quapaws, constitute the Dhegiha linguistic subdivision. The Osages, despite their somewhat peripheral easterly location at the beginning of history, were soon active over wide stretches of the territory occupied by Plains horticulturalists and they had a long history of close contact with the Caddos proper. The Omahas, Poncas, and Kansas have much in common with the Plains horticulturalists, although they exhibit significant variations which will be considered in some detail. These latter groups, as well as the Osages, were scattered in villages along the lower reaches of the rivers draining the Plains and thus held the country commanding the entrance to the eastern border of the main area of Plains horticulture.

In contrast to Siouan, the Caddoan linguistic stock exhibits considerable cultural and traditional uniformity and continuity among its member groups. The constituent languages, while mutually unintelligible, offer no such contrast as that between Catawba, Mandan, and Dakota, say. In their linguistic analysis Lesser and Weltfish list two major divisions of Caddoan. One major division, Caddo, is subdivided into Caddo proper, spoken by some seven tribal units, and Hainai, spoken by three similar divisions. The other major division includes Wichita, spoken by eight bands and a separate language, Kitsai, spoken by one band of the Wichitas; the other group is Pawnee, which has three subdivisions: the South Band dialect, spoken by three distinct bands; the Skiri dialect, spoken by one band; while Arikara constitutes the third subdivision.[6]

All of these Caddoan peoples had been village horticulturalists from ancient times. Their riverine villages were spread along the middle stretches of the rivers of the Plains from South Dakota to eastern Texas. To the south, the Caddos proper are generally considered to deviate from the general pattern of Plains horticulture. The physiography of their territory was not that of the Plains. They are generally presented as being transitional between the culture pattern of the Southeast and that of the Plains. Ample material indicates that the Caddos proper may well prove to be the major hearth from which the fully developed pattern of Plains horticulture derived. On ethnographic distribution maps Osage and Kansa ranges separate the Caddos proper together with the Wichitas from the Pawnees to the north. This is a late movement. As Kroeber notes, the central Kansa territory actually constituted merely the "back country" of the two sedentary Siouan groups.[7] There is archeological proof that the same area was occupied by ancestral Wichita groups in protohistoric times, and there is little doubt that they were in touch with the Caddos proper to the south and the Pawnee groups to the north. Farther north along the Missouri River a westward extension of the Sioux separated the Pawnees and the Arikaras at

[6] Lesser and Weltfish, 1932; Weltfish, 1937, 1965.
[7] Kroeber, 1939, pp. 74, 86; Swanton, 1942, pp. 234–39.

an even later time. At one time the Caddoan-speaking peoples formed virtually a solid block of riverine horticulturalists holding the river bottoms of the eastern Plains from Texas to the Dakotas. As we have seen, archeological research documents this type of riverine horticultural occupation of the central portion of the Plains in prehistoric times, and it seems probable that ancestral Caddoan-speaking peoples carried out the occupation.

The Caddoan-speaking peoples showed a tendency to form political units which could unite their villages into larger, if somewhat ephemeral, units. This trend was strongest among the Caddos proper. In the seventeenth century they are said to have been organized into three or four loose confederacies. Swanton also speaks of a "Wichita Confederation" presumably functioning some time around the beginning of the eighteenth century.[8]

Lesser and Weltfish are in essential agreement with Murie in his claim that the four bands of the Pawnees—Skiri (Wolf, Loup, Panimaha), Pitahawirata (Tappage), Tsawi (Grand), and Kitkahaxki (Republican)—once constituted independent groups. Murie notes, however, that under certain circumstances the Skiri, some thirteen relatively autonomous villages, would consider itself as a "confederacy" in the face of the four or so villages of the combined other bands. Murie's remark that two Skiri villages refused to enter the "confederacy" although they remained on good terms with its members is some indication of the nature of the association.[9] The Arikaras show little evidence of aboriginal confederacies. The early records report them in no more than three or four independent villages com-

[8] Swanton, 1942, pp. 7–16, 59.
[9] Murie, 1914, pp. 549, 551; Dorsey and Murie, 1940, p. 75; Lesser and Weltfish, 1932, p. 4; Weltfish, 1965, p. 5 and passim.

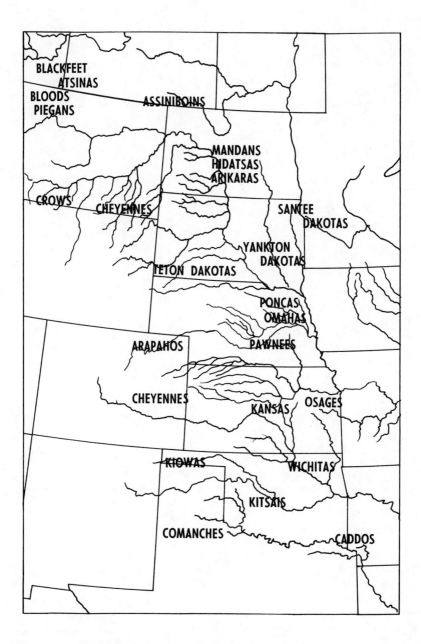

posed of the remnants of some thirty villages which consolidated for mutual protection while retaining separate traditions and claims of autonomy.

Regardless of the shifting, ambiguous nature of any larger federations and alliances, one basic population unit remained both as a central idea and as a physical reality among all of the riverine horticultural peoples: the village. In all the changing circumstances the village as a functioning unit never disappeared. Each riverine horticultural village was a territorially distinct unit of people sharing a common body of speech, tradition, and custom. This group had its own social hierarchy and its own methods of controlling labor, wealth, and prestige. It normally acted as a unit in the face of any outside pressures. Any close affiliation with other such units was based primarily upon linguistic affinity and territorial contiguity, although religious ties might sometimes exist. The physical size of a village appears to have been limited by the available arable land and wood supplies in the river bottoms. As these resources were depleted the location of the village shifted, following a slow cycle of some fifteen to thirty years. The habitations were large, permanent, and, in the north, sod-covered, lodges clustered together in a defensible location, usually on the first or second terrace above the river.

The occupation of these villages was only nominally permanent. Throughout the year the village might be virtually abandoned for considerable periods of time. In the north during the bitter months of winter the people scattered along the river bottoms for some miles in either direction to take up temporary dwelling in sheltered spots.[10] With warmer weather

[10] Boller, 1959, pp. 177–205, gives an excellent eyewitness account of such a settlement in the mid-nineteenth century.

the bison herds returned to the uplands and the raids by enemy groups began again. Thus with the spring the village effected a physical reunion and the people started on the great communal bison hunts to replenish the meat supplies for the coming round of planting ceremonies. Once begun, the horticultural activities gave an integration to all of the activities of the village, even the extended summer communal hunts, an integration which would not be lost until the frosts came in the fall. With the harvest over and food stores laid up, the physical village might once again disintegrate in the face of winter.

This annual cycle must have continued for hundreds of years on the eastern Plains. The villages were an ancient tradition among these people; to understand the pattern of their life one must understand the socio-economic web which held the village together. In any village there was a fundamental interest in stable hierarchical ranking which appears most strikingly in the lives of the men. Essentially there were two groups of men: those with high rank, the leader group; and those without significant rank, the commoners. However, since each man was maintained by the labor of a stable household, and was in effect the representative of the household, it is more accurate to say that any village was divided into leader households and commoner households. Since the household centered around the activities of a family unit, it is also clear that the entire village was divided into leader families and commoner families. The latter phrasing seems to come closest to the view of the people themselves. Not all of the leading families were able to maintain high status through the generations. However, there was a small core of leading families whose rank was assured by religious sanctions and reinforced by economic position, and within that small core there were a few families whose high status was clearly hereditary. Around this high-ranking core there was, through the generations, a fluctuating group of men whose position might be hereditary, or might derive from individual striving, but in any case might never lead to the ranking of their households as leading families. In general, high rank had to be validated by lavish giving and personal achievement, but members of the truly hereditary leading families seem not to have lost status completely even in the absence of validation. On the other hand, the most lavish gift giving and striking personal exploits seem not to have allowed a commoner family to rise to the position of hereditary leader family.[11]

Such structuring is reminiscent of class stratification. However, it must be remembered that the communities were small, the number of people in any status group limited, the lines of stratification somewhat fluid, and the wealth meager. It seems best to speak of nascent classes, stable ranked groups, leader and commoner, rather than the more customary, if less accurate, terms: upper and lower classes, or nobles and commoners.

Since most of the basic data derive from records of the eighteenth and nineteenth centuries, it might be argued that we are here dealing with a late phenomenon deriving out of

[11] This type of social structuring is most readily authenticated for the Pawnees and Arikaras: Dorsey, 1906b; Murie, MS(a), pp. 123–27 and passim; Dorsey and Murie, 1940; Weltfish, 1965, pp. 14–19 and passim; Holder, 1958. But it is also noted for the Mandans in Bowers, 1950, and references to it can readily be found in the early nineteenth-century accounts of European visitors.

European influences. As we will see, the religious sanctions, based as they are on the fundamental activity of horticulture, are of an order to indicate considerable antiquity and would be difficult to derive from late outside sources.

Furthermore, it can be demonstrated from the archeological record that class distinctions of some type extend far back in the prehistoric development of the horticultural way of life in the southeastern United States. Beginning as early as 500 B.C., a series of sedentary horticultural peoples occupied the central valley of the Mississippi River and the country to the east. Accompanying the rise of these cultures was the growth of an intensive ceremonialism which must have involved the total life of the people, their horticulture, and their village organization. These assumptions are based mainly on evidence from ceremonial treatment of the dead.

In the central portions of the Mississippi Valley, about half a millennium before the birth of Christ, a people about whom all too little is known began constructing burial tumuli. The central feature of these monuments was an entombment treated in a fashion to indicate unusually high respect. In addition, objects of considerable rarity and beauty were placed in the mound. There are frequently additional bodies interred in a manner that suggests the sacrifice of retainers, or perhaps some form of suttee. This Hopewell archeological complex and the closely related Adena complex occur sporadically throughout sections of the central valley from this early date until about A.D. 500. The way of life of the ordinary people is little known. Presumably they were horticulturalists, although the precise evidence to support such a contention is scanty. Nor is there abundant evidence of their villages and details of the ordinary aspects of their existence. Mainly we have the impressive

38

evidence of some sort of status difference memorialized in the tumuli and their contents.

Once begun, this veneration of the dead continued. It became more impressive until we find the great temple-mound centers, in the twelfth or thirteenth centuries A.D., of the various Middle Mississippian and related archeological complexes. Here there is always unmistakable evidence that small, select groups of individuals were accorded very special burial treatment. The same complex was still present throughout the southeastern woodlands at the time of De Soto's *entrada*, although the French explorations a century and a half later found only fragments of such a way of life.

The custom of differential treatment of certain of the dead is not of itself proof for the existence of social classes. That proof rests upon an analysis of the setting in which this custom occurs and of the nature of the differential treatment.

The sites where these burials occur are overwhelmingly those which are characterized as ceremonial centers. Associated with the burial grounds are huge earthworks whose construction would demand the organized labor of a great number of workers. The mounds were meticulously formed from individual basket loads of earth into massive pyramidal structures some 100 feet by 800 feet, rising as high as 100 feet and terminating in a platform some 150 feet square. The final mounds appear to be the result of sequential periods of construction according to some sort of calendric cycle, and the man-hours of labor involved in their erection was considerable. Certain burials are marked by the presence of ceremonial paraphernalia found neither in the general debris of the settlement nor with the great majority of burials. These objects differ so completely from other materials yet exhibit such

39

uniformity in style from site to site as to suggest that they were the property of a specially privileged group forming but a restricted segment of the population.[12]

During the first exploration of southeastern North America, De Soto's party noted a stratified society in the large fortified villages along the Mississippi. The French accounts from the later seventeenth century show that this was still the case among the Natchezes, Taensas, Tunicas, Houmas, and other groups along the lower Mississippi River, and among the Caddos to the west. The consistent references to nobility, princes, and ruling classes in the early descriptions are not necessarily nor merely the result of attempts to impose European social standards and patterns in the observations concerning the indigenous peoples.[13]

Among the Caddos proper during the eighteenth century there were close and explicit ties between the priesthood and the nobility. One suspects that the two groups were actually one and that these individuals were in all respects holy. It seems likely that the priesthood served to give religious sanction to the authority which was maintained over the rest of the population. According to the early French and Spanish observers the houses of these people were larger than those of the commoners. The great fire temples were constructed near the house of the *xinesi*, who was by turn head chief and head priest. In some instances this man may have actually lived in the temple. Casañas describes the grand *xinesi*, "like a petty king over them. He holds office by the direct line of descent. If one dies, the nearest blood kin to him becomes his successor. To him are subject . . . nine tribes." He further notes that certain

[12] Waring and Holder, 1945.
[13] Bourne, 1904; Swanton, 1911, 1942.

high seats, or *tepestles*, were reserved for this man and his subordinates. Finally, at public religious ceremonies he spoke with the two sacred children, the holiest of the Caddo religious objects, and fulfilled the functions of a priest.[14]

All of the Caddoan peoples occupied a position peripheral to the main centers of prehistoric horticultural development. On this basis alone one could anticipate that the size of the communities, the amount of surpluses, and the degree of stratification would be less than that at the centers. It seems most likely that the Caddoan peoples of the Plains preserved, in attenuated form, many of the patterns which disappeared in the Mississippi Valley centers sometime during the late sixteenth and early seventeenth centuries.

In the Plains villages of early accounts and ethnographic records the rationale underlying the ordering of interpersonal relations is also related to elements found archeologically in the Mississippi Valley centers. The fundamental supernatural rationale was based ultimately on a system of religious sanctions which were embodied in a physical appurtenance, the sacred village bundle. The bundle is an ancient religious device among North American Indians. It is found widespread as a physical object which contains, and reminds the owner and outsiders of, the supernatural powers controlled by its individual possessor. The logical extension of this principle, whereby

[14] Hidalgo, 1927, p. 51; Casañas, 1927, pp. 213, 215, 290–92. The Spanish reads: "Son de natural apaçibles obedientes a los mandatos de el gran *xinesi*, que es como Reyesuelo de ellos, y este tiene el oficio por linea recta de su linaje que muerto uno entra el que es mas propinque en sanguinidad a el. A este estan sujetos estas nuebe naciones: *Nabadacho* que por otro nombre se llama *Yneci*. . . . [And adds] Este nuebe naciones cogeran de largo, como treinta y cinco leguas, y todas estan sujeta a este gran *xinesi*."

the bundle contains the religious powers of a cooperating group, is more limited in its distribution. Of these two contrasting forms, the personal and the tribal bundle, only the latter will be considered.

There are certain striking analogies between the tribal bundle of the Plains and the ancient ceremonial centers of the Mississippi Valley. One might say figuratively that the bundle was a sort of portable ceremonial center on a much reduced scale. In the ancient centers of the Mississippi Valley the central mounds were often surmounted by a temple which, by historical analogy with such late groups as the Taensa, Natchez, and Caddo Indians and others, was certainly the center of the religious life of the total community. Also just as the tribal bundle among the Arikaras and Pawnees was opened, renewed, and otherwise manipulated within the medicine lodge, so among the groups mentioned baskets and bundles found within the temples were said to serve as a kind of ark, and contained mnemonic devices whose manipulation by the priest ensured the well-being of the community. It is among these groups that the priest seems to have had close ties with or to actually have been the chief.

The Pawnee and Arikara village bundles were the basis for the control of production and of social relations within the villages. The bundle itself was a skin envelope enclosing physical symbols which were used as devices for the recall of complex elements of religious ideology and ritual. The bundle was owned physically by a keeper, who was said to be a lineal descendant of the original owner. It was kept from harm in his house, where it was ministered to and cared for by his wife. On his death it descended to a male relative in the patrilineal line. However, the knowledge associated with the bundle, and the actual manipulation of its contents, was in the charge of a priest who had spent years learning the secrets. In turn, he received compensation for the difficult task of manipulating it and also received gifts from an assistant as he slowly transferred his knowledge. With the transfer of knowledge the priest's power waned until the transmittal of the last bit resulted in his death, whereupon his assistant, usually a close relative, became the new priest.[15]

The continuing life of the village was guaranteed by powers within the bundle, forces derived from a pervasive ocean-of-power investing the universe. The idea is exemplified by the Pawnee term *tirawahut*, so often translated as "God" or "Heaven." A close etymological analysis indicates a meaning nearer to "this which expands" or "this expanse." In this light we can more easily understand the comment offered by the Skiri White Man Chief, on being shown the endless expanse of the Atlantic Ocean: "It was like God."[16]

[15] Murie, 1914, pp. 549–51; Dorsey and Murie, 1940, pp. 75, 77; Lesser, 1933, pp. 107, 111–12. Murie, MS(a), pp. 123–27, gives ample details, which corroborate the others.

[16] White Man Chief's comment will be found in Platt, 1918, p. 789. As with much religious ideology this matter is complex. Weltfish, 1936, p. 49, gives an etymological analysis of *tirawahut* yielding "this expanse," which appears in translation as "Heaven." Murie, MS(a), pp. 42–44 and passim, uses both *Tirawahut* and *Tirawa*, which appears in translation as "God," a usage which is apparently supported by Weltfish, 1965, p. 64: "The supreme god and First Cause was Tirawahat." Grinnell, 1893, p. 114 n 1, gives *Atius*-Father, *Tirawa*-Spirit; but see pp. 121–23 where he gives much the same idea as Weltfish. Later the details are favorably compared with Christian belief, pp. 129–30.

Regardless of these interpretations, the idea of an incorporeal power surcharging the universe was present; Murie, MS(a), passim, but especially pp. 130–51 in connection with bundle renewals, where it is often mentioned also as "Luck." There is abundant reference to the same idea among the Arikaras.

The power came to the people through the bundle by virtue of the intercession of the priests and hereditary chiefs. According to Lesser's report of their secret sessions, the Pawnee Chief's Society believed that it was they who had given the bundles to the people and designated priests who could manipulate and explain these devices. The chiefs considered themselves to be stars on earth. The arrangement of the ceremony in their society was a mirror reflection of the astronomical charts expounded by the priesthood. Although a chief validated his political position through his own behavior to maintain authority in the council of elder men, he could lose only his political status. No chief lost his real rank; a deposed chief would remain a member of a leading family. The secrecy of some of the details concerning the chiefs' powers suggests that these leaders felt no need to validate their position by overt demonstrations of their superior status.[17]

The hereditary chiefs were charged with the administrative task of maintaining the status quo in the village and assuring that problems which arose were handled by the proper agencies. Not only were the chiefs said to be stars on earth but they were also, in a manner of speaking, the earthly reservoirs of a power which enabled them to be the father and protector of their children, the people. The chief should never participate in personal violence within the village. There was little call for him to take an active part in the military adventures of the raiding parties; leadership in such activities was entrusted to

[17] Weltfish, 1965, p. 272. Lesser's comments are from my notes on a lecture given in seminar at Columbia University in the mid-1930s. For other details see especially Murie, MS(a), which has several illustrations of the Pawnee star-charts, with explanatory notes; Fletcher, 1904; Buckstaff, 1927; Dorsey and Murie, 1940, p. 77.

ranking warriors. A leader thus appointed was not so much a "war chief" as a trusted brave who honored the chief by functioning as his proxy in a situation which might unduly threaten the physical security of the village head. Nevertheless, details of the launching and field conduct of such campaigns remained under the strict surveillance of the chief.

The role of the war leader is illustrated by an episode from Long's exploration of the Missouri Valley in the early 1800s. One of Long's groups had been robbed by some Pawnee (Republican) raiders who had got out of the control of their leader. Subsequently the Pawnee villagers, as well as the Omahas, Iowas, Otos, Missouris, and others, sent delegates to Long's council at Engineer's Cantonment. One of the matters facing the Pawnees on Long's agenda was the theft:

They arrived about noon, seventy in number, consisting of individuals of each of the three tribes, called Grand Pawnees, Pawnee Republicans, and Pawnee Loups, or Panimahas, and halted some distance from our camp. As we approached them we noticed the majority of them standing in a forest of young willow trees, holding their mules by the bridles, and looking dubiously around. The chief of the principal band, Long Hair, was haranguing them in a loud voice. "Take off your saddles; why do you stand peeping and trembling in the bushes? You ought to have trembled when the whites were seen near the Kansa villages." [18]

This leader was brave in the face of danger. He demonstrated his superiority over his followers by his example, as well as by choosing just that time to embarrass them. He indicated his position of unquestioned authority and bravery not only to the

[18] James, 1905, vol. 14, p. 240. See also Murray, 1839, vol. 1, pp. 278–84.

Americans but also to the other tribes, many of whom were potential or actual enemies. There can be no doubt of the administrative perspicacity of this man or of his confidence in the power which bolstered his position.

In any matter involving the village as a whole the chief was the leader. It was no fiction that the chiefs were the life forces of the bundle-transferred power which enabled the village to continue as an integrated unit. The people firmly believed that the loss or "death" of the bundle would mean the death of the people. This was no idle belief. The loss of the bundle would mean the end of the religio-political ordering which maintained the chief and held the people together under him. The success of all enterprises, individual and cooperative, flowed from the village bundle via the medium of the priest and chief. Thus they were supported by the community and held in high respect. The priests were the custodians and professors of the body of religious lore. No member of the community was barred access to the knowledge essential for handling the power of the bundle, but since the apprenticeship was lengthy and required gifts, the office tended to fall into the hands of leader families with the needed resources.[19]

In keeping with their position the priests and chiefs followed a personality pattern which is almost a stereotype. They were men to whom violence was a stranger; they were quiet and secure in the knowledge of their power. Their voices were never raised in anger or threatened violence. The image was one of large knowledge, infinite quiet patience, and thorough understanding. There was no outward show of authority; such was not needed. During Long's tour James noted the "lofty

[19] Murie, MS(a), pp. 122–25, has interesting details.

dignity" of a Grand Pawnee chief's appearance: "But his extreme hauteur became manifest when he halted at the head of our line, but not offering his hand or even deigning to look at us." [20] These were secure, calm, well-bred, gracious men whose largesse was noted and who had no need to shout of their strength.

The deliberations of the council of elders were under the charge of the village chief acting for the leader families. Throughout the year there were also many ceremonies and religious gatherings at which this group presided through their representatives, the priests, and, by proxy, through the chiefs. In these meetings the integrating function of the bundle was made manifest to the people. With the coming of spring the bundles were taken from their resting places and renewed. Awakened from their winter sleep, they needed the sun to fertilize them with the magic forces that would lead the village through the coming seasons. Unless this ceremony was performed the world would die. Only the priests could perform it. Somewhat earlier the great communal winter bison hunt had been undertaken with due ceremony to obtain meat for the planting rituals. A captive virgin might be taken by some man seeking to raise his standing. She would be brought to the village and sacrificed at the end of the long fertility rituals of the Morning Star. The importance of fertility rites with the accompanying practice of human sacrifice and ritual cannibalism is well attested for Pawnee groups of the nineteenth century. The Arikaras of the same period followed a similar practice. We may assume from the religious context that the complex is aboriginal and ancient. Persistent reports of cannibalism among

[20] James, 1905, vol. 14, p. 149.

the Caddos proper of the eighteenth century, as well as among the Wichitas, may be seen as references to this ceremonial fertility complex.[21]

The communal bison hunts of the summer growing season were conducted with much solemn ceremony, as were the fall festival of the harvest and the great Twenty Day ceremony. During the latter the theatrical performances of the doctors with their feats of legerdemain, their sorcery duels, and other dramatic performances would focus the village inward for weeks on end. All of these annual ceremonies were under the aegis of the supernatural powers of the universe and their earthly representatives.

This recurring round of ceremonies and feasts gave the village a continuing integrity in the eyes of the people. There were also occasions when, as individuals, the people could come into personal contact with the powers: the spring bene-diction performed over each woman's seed-corn cache; the priestly validation of the vision which led a rising young parti-san to plan a guerilla raid; the long sessions at which a neophyte memorized the rituals of the priest or a similar initiate slowly learned the secrets of an animal lodge of the doctors. These

[21] Such references include those of: Penicaut in Margry, 1876–88, vol. 5, pp. 502–4. Swanton, 1942, pp. 188–89. De Mézières and Gaignard in Bolton, 1914, vol. 1, pp. 286, 289; vol. 2, p. 85. James, 1905, vol. 15, pp. 152–53. Irving, 1935, vol. 1, pp. 140–44. School-craft, 1851, p. 614; 1853, pt. 5, pp. 77 ff.; vol. 6, pp. 495–96. Later comments are found in: Dorsey, 1906a; Wissler and Spinden, 1916; Linton, 1923a, 1926. Murie, MS(a), has a wealth of rich detail and must be consulted for a thorough evaluation of the ceremony, especially the accompanying songs as retranslated by Weltfish (pp. 405–537). Weltfish, 1965, pp. 482, 106–18, 467, and passim, has abundant ethnographic detail and reviews the literature.

individual encounters were charged with mystic power, but it was the great communal feasts which focused life in the village and fitted the more random experiences into a larger well-planned whole.

Associated with all ritual activities were lesser posts, the filling of which might give a man modest and secure status throughout life. Although these men—waiters, fire tenders, and criers—did not actually partake of the glory of the leaders, they basked in a sort of reflected light. They might become intimate with all of the stages of a ritual and know in an unofficial way many of the secrets, but they would never be able to use that knowledge for their own ends. These positions were held in considerable regard and tended to be handed down from father to son as an avenue by which some commoners of the village might find niches for themselves.

Additional ladders of personal achievement were open to the common men of the village. The hierarchical association of the doctors was an extremely important means by which a man might gain status and prestige. The curing techniques practiced by the doctors were basically those of the familiar North American shaman. These practices are so widespread that they undoubtedly have a long history of development. Among the village peoples the pattern of forming complex, stratified organizations was extended to the activities of the doctors. Among the Arikaras, for example, the outward appurtenance of the system was a series of animal lodges, or societies. The curing knowledge which each lodge controlled was derived from its tutelary animal or group of animals whose name was used to designate the specific lodge. Membership in any lodge could come through various channels: by request, after being cured by a lodge member, because one was marked by the tutelary animal before birth, or because one's close relatives belonged.[22]

Given the necessary time and wealth, a man could learn the curing knowledge and attendant public mummery of lodge after lodge until he was finally in possession of the total body of knowledge. This fitted him for association with the small group of doctors known as the Leader Lodge. From their seats on the altar these men controlled all of the members and neophytes of the constituent lower lodges. Not only were payments made to the lodge to which one belonged, but each lodge made gifts and payments to the Leader Lodge. The leading doctors were men of considerable means.

All doctors of any repute were banded together in this animal lodge association. Curers or sorcerers who operated outside of it did so as individuals and as such were considered to be less powerful. In the lower ranks, of course, there were many lodge members who could not be considered shamans or curers in any sense.

In theory, the doctors were supposed to be circumspect and quiet in public life. They were to use their curing powers for the benefit of the village. Descriptions of the actual behavior of the doctors, however, indicate a divergence between theory and practice. Not only did they resort to threats and intimidation in order to bolster their position, they also brandished in-group sorcery as their most powerful weapon. Exhibitionistic sorcery duels, given during the great Twenty Day ceremony among the Pawnees, demonstrated to the people that these men dealt with death as well as curing, that they would dra-

[22] Grinnell, 1893; Curtis, 1909; Wissler and Spinden, 1916; Murie, 1914; Murie, MS(a); Linton, 1923b; Gilmore, 1931; Weltfish, 1965, pp. 203–309.

Karl Bodmer

A Mandan Dandy

Karl Bodmer

A Nomad Camp

Karl Bodmer

A Winter Village

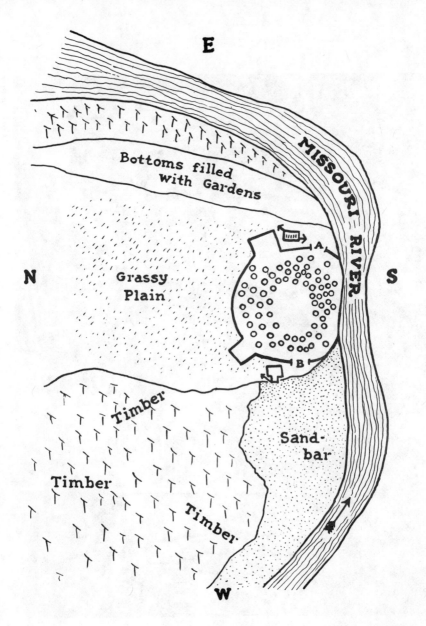

E

MISSOURI RIVER

Bottoms filled
with Gardens

N

Grassy
Plain

A

S

B

Timber

Timber

Timber

Sand-
bar

W

Gilbert L. Wilson

An Earth-lodge Village

Karl Bodmer

In an Earth Lodge

Karl Bodner

A Mandan Buffalo Dance

Karl Bodmer

A Buffalo Hunt

Karl Bodmer

A Raid at Fort McKenzie

matically cure the very disorders which they themselves could inflict.

An examination of the basic rationale underlying the religion helps to understand how the activities of the doctors could be sanctioned, how it came about that their antisocial acts were tolerated by the village. There is a deeply ingrained dualism running through the religious ideology of the Caddoan-speaking peoples. Essentially this dualism was a structuring of the actual processes of nature and as such was not morally toned. There were and must be forces of reproduction and disintegration, elements of construction and destruction, magic powers of life and of death. The two large divisions of the annual cycle corresponding to summer and winter, and based on celestial observation, express this dualism: the period of growth when the magic forces lived and acted, and the remainder of the year when they were dormant. Not only did the power reveal itself in the complexities of sky beings, but also the animals and the earthly forces were seen as polar counterparts of the celestial powers.

Just as the chiefs were sky figures come to earth, the doctors were earth figures who partook of power through the medium of earthly animals. The chiefs and priests were figures concerned with life in all of its aspects: the miracle of reproduction, the growing of crops, the perpetuation of village life. By contrast the doctors in their activities were associated with death and the forces of destruction. Their curing may be best understood as a technique for holding off the forces of death, which at any time they might release by their own volition.

The religious sanctions for the animal lodges and the activities of the doctors were derived from animal powers

51

contained in the village bundle. These animals express the basic dualism as an earthly manifestation of the ocean-of-power, at the same time less powerful but direr than the celestial manifestations. The differentiation of earth and sky powers is indicated in the final act of the Morning Star sacrifice on the scaffold. As the captive climbs the "animal power" rungs of wolf, wildcat, panther, and bear, symbolized by skins on the willow withes, a running song by the priests indicates that these rungs also symbolize, in order, cloud power, wind power, lightning power, and thunder power.[23]

Another aspect of the dualism was the fact that although the doctors might practice in-group sorcery, it was powerless against the chief and priest. These latter men seem also to have had access to powers of sorcery, although there are hints that it was primarily for out-group aggression. It is also clear that this power could "tangle up the mind of a doctor" and cause his untimely death were he brash enough to attack a priest or a chief.[24]

Although a man might raise himself to the top of the doctor hierarchy, he could never by this means quite attain the position and prestige accorded the beneficent life figures of the village. In the peoples' eyes he contrasted with those silent, secure individuals who functioned for the good of the group. The stereotype for the doctors was that of a grasping, fat, foul-smelling death figure who spent his life bleeding the people for his own ends, a man who would finally die through his very association with the death-dealing powers that allowed him to climb to the heights.

[23] Murie, MS(a), pp. 427–28.
[24] For the Arikaras, Tabeau, 1939, pp. 136, 185; the Wichitas, Curtis, 1930, p. 60; the Omahas, Fortune, 1932; the Pawnees, Murie, MS, and Weltfish, 1965, pp. 332–46.

There were other paths of personal achievement open to even the poorest of the orphan boys, and there were long years in which one might work at these achievements, since maturity was considered to come late to Pawnee and Arikara men. Much leeway was permitted in the behavior of men under forty years of age, in the group where we find the Boys. A chief's son thirty or so years old might be considered so unstable, wild, and "unchiefly" in his behavior that he would be unable to accept and fulfill the heavy responsibilities of the chieftainship. In this event a regent might be appointed to serve until the youngster of thirty became a mature man. At that time, as the true chief, he would assume his obligations and discharge them without embarrassment to himself or his people.

Young men of leader families, as well as the other Boys, could act in a fashion unbecoming to an older man. The Boys were wild and irresponsible and many of their acts were irresponsible. Nevertheless, the opinion of the older men and the established authorities carried weight with these young men. They could not escape the prestige of the village bundle in the background. It was rather that wild behavior which did no serious damage to the village came more often from the Boys than from any other group.

Among the Boys was the Plains dandy, a young man on his way up by whatever means was at hand, spending his free time in eternal gambling games, dancing, and bragging; one who gave endless attention to personal appearance—beard plucking, tonsures, and paints; who wore striking costumes and indulged in endless nervous comings and goings.[25]

[25] Of the many descriptions in the early literature none surpasses the graphic detail given by Maximilian, 1906, vol. 23, pp. 258–65, among the Mandans of the 1830s. Murray, 1839, vol. 1, p. 150 and passim, more briefly does much the same for the Pawnees at about the same time.

The category Boy was not only an approximately age-graded classification; it was also a social category that might include many full-grown men who were, in effect, declassed, or who had never been able to move out of this lower rank of men. The Boys formed the reservoir from which recruits were drawn for military expeditions. The responsibility for preserving the village in actual attack by outsiders was given the Boys, and they obtained wealth for the village by raiding outside groups under partisan leadership. Both of these activities were organized into a system granting prestige to those individuals who took an active part in warfare. In the lives of those whose status was secure the war ladder might play little part. The chiefs and priests were virtually prohibited from taking part in offensive warfare, and the doctors did not need to fight with physical weapons.

War activities, whether of a defensive or an offensive nature, were sanctioned by the bundle. The partisan who felt moved to raid the enemy as a result of some personal hallucinatory experience nevertheless sought out the priest to obtain the blessing of the bundle needed for his expedition. In return for the blessing there would be gifts to the priest and ultimately to the chief, who had ensured the success of the expedition in their official capacities. If the raid was a failure it was the partisan who had failed to observe the proper precautions. As for the Boys whom the partisan recruited by holding out rewards of increased prestige, their lot was the bulk of the effort and the least of the returns.

To honor the bundle the successful partisan might "put up" a feast during which he gave gifts to the bundle as a token of his gratitude. These gifts were part of the loot which had funneled up to him from the members of his raiding party, as well as his own possessions. Such presents might also be made directly to the village chief to honor him as a surrogate for the whole group; or they could find their way to the chief indirectly through the priest, again in the context of honoring.

The dancing fraternities were the main avenue of achievement for the Boys. Although they were secular organizations, some were sanctioned by the bundle. Many were invented by individuals through dreams and visions without ever receiving formal religious sanction. The fraternities were graded; those sanctioned by the bundle were considered to be more prestigious and membership within them tended to be hereditary. However, an individual might join one or all of them in any order, provided he came by the wealth which was needed to pay his way through the ranks.[26]

These fraternities lacked the aura of sanctity which was attached to the chiefs' and priests' activities. They were primarily mundane social clubs which held certain special dances and activities at various times, analogous to similar fraternal orders in our own society, even to the extent that an individual who joined many of them did not necessarily have high prestige but might only be considered a "joiner."

In addition to the purely exhibitionistic side of their activities the fraternities functioned in a socially constructive manner for the total village. A given fraternity might aid the women in work around the village. Fraternities might act as coordinated units in the communal bison hunts or in warfare, and on many occasions a fraternity might be given the responsibility of policing the village or the camp. They retained their mundane character, however, and membership in them was insufficient to raise an individual's prestige to the level of that of the

[26] Murie, 1914; Lowie, 1916, p. 115.

members of the leader families. Even though the various activities of the Boys were socially useful, whether in hunting, warfare, or the day-to-day tasks of the village, their status-striving efforts were always stopped short of the positions of the hereditary leaders. At most they could hope to gain the position of successsful warrior and, with luck, achieve the post of top-ranking brave.[27]

These were the major roads of life for the men in the horti-cultural villages: To be born a member of the hereditary leader families meant to slip into the position of chief or of priest or to raise oneself through the animal lodges until one became a great, threatening doctor. The commoners could travel along the war road, climb the lesser ladder of the dancing fraternities, and become a brave, or remain among the ranks of the insignificant with the other Boys. It is little wonder that there was occasional rebellious behavior on the part of the Boys and that at a later date it sometimes threatened the integrity of the village as a cooperating unit.

The structure is here idealized. The social compartments were not neat and mechanical. What is important is that any aberrant shifting from category to category was not frequent enough to threaten the basic functioning of the community.

The labor which maintained the village was communal in the sense that its results went to support the entire village member-ship; products were shared by all. This is not to imply that the majority of the tasks were carried out by the village en masse as a single cooperating group. It was rather that the more or less autonomous units which made up the village directed their individual tasks toward common goals at specific times.

[27] De Mézières notes much the same pattern among the Wichitas of the late eighteenth century; Bolton, 1914.

The basic unit was a type of expanded family with a specific earth lodge as its focal point through time. Such an ideal unit consisted of some fifteen to twenty persons under the leadership of a middle-aged woman whose lodge and attendant fields provided a secure base for the group. There were three generations united in their affectual ties by bonds of marriage and descent, with a weighting on the distaff side. In the elder generation was the woman lodge builder with her spouse, and occasional associated age mates. The next generation was represented by a group of daughters or, in some instances, sons, with their in-marrying spouses and other, more distant kin. The third generation was composed of the children of the middle group. The elderly woman controlled the destiny of the household. She had much to say regarding the activities of all members. Her husband appears to have been concerned with reliving past glories, partaking in status-raising activities among the men, and serving as a mentor for the children. The bond between grandparent and grandchild was stronger than that between parent and child. The grandmother-leader appears to have been given the emotional ties which in our society are received by the actual mother.[28]

The major load of work was carried by the middle group of people, twenty to fifty years of age. They were the actual

[28] Weltfish, 1965, offers full details among the Pawnees, especially pp. 20–37. Lesser, 1930, gives marriage patterns. Eggan, 1952, 1966, with his students, the Schmitts; Lounsbury, 1956; and Deetz, 1965, leaning heavily on Eggan and associates, have all speculated on variations in the form, showing special concern with the matrilineal weighting. Benedict's statement (1923, p. 56), "Among the Arikara of the Plains, descent was maternal in a characteristic clan setting (Goddard and Reichard Field Notes)," may have awakened such interest. Her claim for clans is not supported by later field work.

productive core of the household. This group carried out its activities along lines sharply demarcated by a sexual division of labor which extended through the entire village fabric. As a result of their affinal ties, the in-marrying group of men were responsible, aside from ceremonial activities, for duties which lay outside the intimate life of the lodge. They were mainly hunters, charged with the task of providing meat for the household, and they were, of course, responsible for the military protection of the village.

The women were concerned with basic tasks which held the lodge together as a continuing entity. They were interested in the maintenance of a permanent dwelling, the care of children, the production of staple vegetable foods, and the preservation of all types of provender. They processed skins and furs and manufactured clothing, basketry, and pottery. They owned, controlled, and worked the lands. From them came the really basic foodstuffs and surpluses and, in consequence, all of the essentially permanent fixtures of life. Their actual position in the society must have been strong, since their work was the basic guarantee against the dissolution of the villages.

The women had functioning roles in all of the important ceremonies. They had their own sororities and societies with their own special dances and rituals. When a neophyte sat at the feet of a priest or a doctor among the Arikaras to learn the secrets, his wife sat with him, "in order that he might never forget." By this process the women had access to many of the secrets. As we have seen, among the Pawnees the physical care of the bundle was in the hands of a woman.[29]

This position for women seems to have been true for all the Caddoan-speaking peoples. Solis, in the 1760s, speaks of a

[29] Murie, 1914, pp. 555–56; Holder, Arikara Field Notes.

great or principal lady among the southern Caddos (Tejas) to whom the entire nation brought gifts and who he says had five husbands: "In short she is like a queen among them." At about the same time Morfi noted that among the Wichitas the government was "democratic, without the exclusion of women." The French observer de Mézières makes similar comments for the same period.[30]

The religion was threaded with basic concepts which reveal high status and a position of authority for women as well as high prestige for the female role in general. The bundles were called "Mother," and they might have such names as Mother Born Again or Lucky Woman Leader. The basic dualism of Caddoan religion was also expressed in sexual terms. The Evening Star was the female counterpart of the male Morning Star. The planted corn seeds in their mound of earth were female, awaiting fertilization by the male rain. The resultant crop came from a union of the male sky and the female earth. The importance of the Mother Corn in the religion is a reflection of the actual importance of the corn reserves and their female producers.

As the village continued its unity through time, so the lodge units had continuity and held together the kin-nuclei which were, in effect, the basic building blocks forming the foundation of the village. The status ranking which has been outlined with respect to individuals was a reflection of a relative ranking of the households within the village. Family lines maintained this ranking through time. Individuals were not only leaders or commoners; more essentially, they were members of leader or

[30] Solis, 1931, p. 61; Morfi, 1935, pt. 1, p. 66; Bolton, 1914, vol. 2, p. 203; Tabeau, 1939, p. 178. Trudeau, 1914, pp. 457–61 gives details from the Arikaras.

commoner family lines. Not only did supernatural sanctions descend along inheritance lines, but also such families were in a position, because of the nature of economic exchange in the village, to be just those with the resources essential for the feasts and gift giving needed to validate the high name of their children. These children would then become the high-ranking leaders of the village. There was a strong tendency toward class endogamy; a commoner could hardly enter into the arranged marriages of the higher ranks. Leading families among the Pawnees not only had access to sacred or esoteric lore, but also retained control of such things by marriages within the family. Apparently the basic emotional warmth noted above allowed a special intimacy and potential marriage ties with the real or the classificatory grandparent group. Since this classificatory group involved a close collateral line descending from the actual grandparent, control of knowledge would thus be focused within the leader family and its immediate branches.[31] Through time, therefore, the village tended to be sorted into the "haves" and the "have-nots."

In the late nineteenth-century village of Like-a-Fishhook, the Arikara lodges, as later identified by informants who had once lived there, were sorted on the basis of the social status of the families. The leading families lived in larger lodges near the center of the village, while the commoner families were in smaller dwellings along the outer edge. It is not clear whether this ranking was reflected in and related to the productive

[31] Lesser, 1933, p. 42, on the basis of field work, is specific concerning attempts at control. Lounsbury, 1956, speculates on the marriage possibilities, while Weltfish, 1965, pp. 22–26, delineates the kinship lines and supports the whole matter with statements from informants, although she does not mention Lounsbury's guesses.

capacities of the various family units. A suggestion of such a differential is found in the fact that the chief allotted the use of units of arable land to the families on the basis of need. A high-ranking family might well require richer or more extensive fields in order to fulfill its obligation to the group. Murie notes that at the time of distribution of land on the Pawnee reservation in Oklahoma, the farms were parceled out by the chiefs according to the needs of the families in the following descending order: chiefs, priests, doctors, warriors (braves), soldiers, and commoners.[32]

The mechanism which assured the distribution of village wealth was an elaboration of the familiar North American aboriginal idea that hospitality and giving are the hallmark of high status. On the basis of this practice the products of the village constantly flowed between family units and were dispersed throughout the community to assure even the lowliest family of subsistence. A series of feasts or ceremonial activities in which the whole village participated was the main channel along which the wealth flowed. There were many times when family units themselves gave gifts and feasts, but the important socially recognized mechanism was the ceremonial feast.

Throughout the socio-economic framework of the village the signposts all read, "Give!" This was a sharing sort of giving and its basic rationalization was as deeply rooted in the cultural milieu as is our idea of self-aggrandisement and display. One gave to increase and ensure the security of the whole group. One gave to increase one's own prestige and the security and future prestige of one's children and kin. One gave to ensure good crops and successful hunting. And above all, one kept on

[32] Dorsey and Murie, 1940, pp. 97–100; Murie, MS(a); Holder, Arikara Field Notes.

good terms with the supernatural and assured oneself of a long life by giving the very real necessities of life. There was a recurring phrase, "It is hard to be a chief," which contains the essence of the reality that there were few chiefs and many commoners. In order to maintain one's high status, goods must constantly be given downward along the ladder of prestige. There were few families possessing the facilities to withstand the drain on their resources. It was only by feasts and entertainments, with the attendant gift giving to all guests, that a person validated and maintained his position in the social scale.

By analogy with gift-giving practices among nomadic groups of the Plains, this type of distribution system among the horticulturalists could reflect a basically democratic and thoroughgoing redistribution of wealth. The mechanism of redistribution actually functioned among the northern Caddoan horticulturalists with a flaw in the sharing principle. The basic key lies in the relative ranking within the village, and in the distinctive nature of the downward giving. Throughout the social structure as progressively higher status levels were reached, more and more individuals were giving to fewer and fewer in the upward stream. Not only must all commoners give upward to the leaders, but the leaders also gave upward toward the peak of the pyramid within their own group. Thus goods funneled toward those on the very top: the head chief, the head priest, and the head doctors. This funneling was manifest in the public ceremonies where all, participant or spectator, contributed to the good of the group by giving wealth to the leaders of the ceremony.

The cultural ideal demanded that this upward giving be accorded an honorific aura; one gave upward that which one considered to be dearest. As Casañas early noted among the

Caddos, "The respect and obedience they show the grand *xinesi* is remarkable. Everybody tries to keep him satisfied by giving him something of everything he has and by going out to hunt something for him to feast upon." [33] Those who were of higher status than the giver deserved only the best. In his greatest sacrifice the giver partook of the recipient's greatness. This idea was constantly reinforced by public opinion. One who gave upward with tight fingers was open to public censure.

The other side of the coin is somewhat different. Not everything came back down through the status levels. There was, of course, a rigidly enforced custom that there must be giving downward. A chief who was not generous would not long retain the good will of his constituents, without which he was powerless. Priests and doctors were under less pressure by the very nature of their activities. Giving downward generally occurred at public ceremonies or gatherings. Any gathering, religious or secular, was accompanied by a feast at which basic foodstuffs were distributed to all present. There was, in addition, a complex series of formal religious observances in which the feasts were accompanied by the giving away of surplus goods. On these latter occasions the goods were contributed by all who attended, and the principle was in force of giving one's choice objects—bison robes, deerskins, decorated clothing, moccasins, and other choice items. These goods were presented directly to the leaders of the ceremony in their capacity as surrogates for the powers being invoked on the occasion. In reality the gifts became the property of the leaders. At the conclusion of the ceremony the leaders demonstrated their high status by redistributing the goods to all present, retaining only

[33] Casañas, 1927, p. 218.

some items for their own use. The principle of choice still held in the downward giving, but it now functioned in reverse for the contributors. Since only the best was good enough for the highest, then as the goods were redistributed, the best must be retained in descending order through the ranks of all of those present. This reassortment of wealth was publicly sanctioned and as rigidly enforced as the opposite principle. The lowest contributed their best and received the least.

In order to maintain their position the upper ranks had to control enough wealth to validate that position, since their primary economic function was to control the flow of wealth and redistribute goods. However, the society was so structured as to ensure that the upper ranks alone had access to the means which were needed to demonstrate high status. They grandly gave away goods which funneled up to them. The flow never ceased, for if it had, there would have been no stable upper ranks. The whole ceremonial round demanded the presence of such an upper rank to whom gifts were given. The cessation of the hereditary leading families or the gifts would have meant, in effect, the cessation of the entire ceremonial life of the village, and thereby of the village itself.

As suggested before, there was an additional avenue for the circulation of wealth: the payments which were made in graduating through the ranks of the various hierarchical organizations. These payments were not thought of as gifts. There was no demand for return gifts where knowledge was exchanged for goods. In these organizations again there were many exchanging their wealth, now for knowledge that was still controlled by few. In the important organizations one had to make payment after payment to a preceptor who taught, little by little, the secrets which gave one the power to control ceremonial knowledge. The native idea that there were always few chiefs and many commoners stood on real economic facts.

Not only, therefore, was the horticultural village an ancient reality on the Plains, but also these villages were socially stratified and were economically autonomous with resources channeled inward to maintain the status lines. The term "autonomous" does not imply a lack of trade relations between villages. The widespread calumet pipe ceremony so often reported in early historical accounts is one indication of extensive intergroup relations on the prehorse Plains. This well-integrated religious rite cemented peaceful relations between groups along the lines of fictional kin ties in combination with an exchange of goods. The antiquity of the custom is supported by its wide distribution, its set ritual, and by specific mid-seventeenth-century Sioux traditions regarding its origins among the "Panis." It seems likely that the rise and spread of such a custom was a necessary accompaniment of both trade and warfare.[34]

The historical and ethnological data concerning the nature of intergroup activities will be examined below. The intensification of these relations in historic times must be seen, however, as the end product of a long process of indigenous development on the eastern Plains with an attendant increase in their complex ties, especially following the introduction of European influences into the New World.

[34] Mentions of the ceremony include those of Allouez (1667) in Kenton, 1927, vol. 2, p. 172; Jolliet and Marquette (1673) in Kellogg, 1917, pp. 246–47; Perrot in Blair, 1911, vol. 1, pp. 182–86; Delisle and Michel, résumé of Joutel (1687) in Margry, 1876–88, vol. 3, pp. 404–6, 415–19; Celiz (1718–19), 1935, pp. 73–76; La Harpe (1719) in Margry, 1876–88, vol. 6, p. 290. See also Fletcher, 1904.

This idealized abstraction reduces the way of life of the peoples involved to its basic pattern. The nature of the aboriginal society was reconstructed from historical accounts and ethnographic records, as they were illuminated by archeological research. The records come from a period filled with change brought about by European contacts and the subsequent rise of the equestrian nomads. Yet the pattern which has been abstracted exhibits inner consistency and richness; it is a picture of a functioning culture without reference to the horse complex.[35]

The ancient pattern was one of fairly self-sufficient villages, each with its web of socio-economic relations which assured traditional continuity, stability, and a thorough channeling and limitation of innovations. Society stood tied to the earth. Corn was its protector. The fields of the river bottoms were its insurance in the face of a difficult environment. The labor of the village and the rewards of life were focused in these fields. The whole was woven into a fabric which continued through time.

This complex must be seen in relation to those of neighboring

[35] In addition to sources cited and my own field observations, I have consulted passim with varying degrees of success: Morgan, 1871a, 1871b, pp. 291–382; Grinnell, 1889, 1891a, 1891b, 1892, 1893, 1894; Fletcher, 1900, 1904; Dorsey, 1902, 1904a, 1904b, 1904c, 1905, 1906b, 1906c, 1906d, 1906e; Wissler, 1915, 1920; Linton, 1922; Gilmore, 1925a, 1925b, 1926a, 1926b, 1927, 1928, 1930, 1931; Weltfish, 1936, 1937, 1965. However, as with my field notes, some of the material is as yet unpublished. I have been fortunate in having access to the bulk of the unpublished Murie manuscripts, "The Ceremonies of the Pawnee," on file, Bureau of American Ethnology, and "Skiri Pawnee Texts," on file, Department of Anthropology, American Museum of Natural History. See Weltfish, 1965, pp. 480–83, for a very authoritative evaluation and use of these manuscripts, as well as a thorough review of extant sources on the Pawnees.

areas. Some of its variations must be understood, specifically those of some of the sedentary Siouan peoples. The relation of all these villages to the outside world, which would change rapidly with the appearance of Europeans and the equestrian nomads on the Plains, must be first defined in the light of relations between the horticultural groups themselves.

The most obvious conflicts and rivalries on the native Great Plains of the nineteenth century centered about the polar distinction between settled people and nomadic groups, between the horticultural groups and the mounted hunters. Similar conflicts are familiar to us from our own historical traditions. In the Old World the struggle between settled farmers along the rivers of the Middle East and elsewhere, on the one hand, and the pastoral nomads on the other, is an old and familiar story. That it should be repeated in analogous form on the Great Plains of North America so late in mankind's history is one indication of the kinds of regularities that recur in the gamut of culture change. But the similarities must be seen also as being in some respects superficial and above all as deriving from fundamentally different historical roots. The fact that the horse as a means of transportation was shared by both areas should not obscure the fact that the nomads of the New World were in no sense of the word pastoralists in the same fashion as those of the Old World. The way of life of the New World nomads and details of their conflict with the horticultural people will be delineated below. But first some differences and conflicts between the village peoples themselves must be examined in some detail.

Archeological evidence indicates stability of village life for hundreds of years along the eastern fringes of the Plains and the wooded bottoms of the permanent streams threading their way out of the western mountain massif. This stability is likely to have endured had it not been for the introduction of new peoples and ideas from the Old World. Nevertheless, the native way of life was never uniform. Differentiation among the horticulturalists must have come from ancient roots.

The variant horticulturalists of our concern belong to the Siouan linguistic stock. It has been seen that the Siouans vary greatly in their historical background and cultural orientation. In the north the Mandans and Hidatsas have more in common with the northern Caddoans than with the Siouan Dakotas, their neighbors.[36] The Mandans first appear in history during the fourth decade of the eighteenth century, settled along the middle reaches of the Missouri River. Desultory reports continue, and the next century opens with abundant records from the visits, in sequence, of David Thompson, Lewis and Clark, Alexander Henry, Larocque, and others to their well-known villages below the Knife River. The Mandans had for some time been associated with recently migrant groups identified by various authorities as the Hidatsas and affiliated enclaves.[37] At the nearby Fort Clark villages they were later visited by the acute observer Maximilian, Prince of Wied-Neuwied, as well as George Catlin, just before the terrible smallpox epidemic which caught them in their earth lodges during the spring and summer of 1837, reducing their numbers from some twelve hundred to fewer than twenty survivors. Their ethnic autonomy was thus ended, and ethnological observations after that time are

[36] Voegelin, 1941; Voegelin and Voegelin, 1964, p. 114; and Wolff, 1950, review the salient linguistic data.

[37] Bowers, 1965, pp. 10–25, discusses at length the confusing and conflicting early reports and attempts to verify some of the information from living informants. Consultation of the original sources is also advisable.

garnered from a relict group ultimately living as a minor group within the Hidatsa villages.

An accurate reconstruction of the Mandans' old way of life has been an extremely difficult task. In effect a series of traditions are remembered and retold by a people already much mixed with their heterogeneous neighbors, the Hidatsas.[38] They originally formed a relatively small group of horticulturalists living near the confluence of the Heart and the Missouri and later of the Knife and the Missouri.[39] Earlier settlements were downstream where La Vérendrye heard of eight villages in 1733.[40] In later times they were settled in only three villages, one of at least 113 lodges. Two associated villages

[38] As Lowie, 1917, p. 7, puts it: "The study of ancient Mandan society is rendered unusually difficult through the almost complete extinction of the tribe. There are probably not more than half a dozen full-blood Mandan living . . . if we could be sure that recently collected Mandan data . . . reflect ancient Mandan conditions. Unfortunately, we are frequently without the means of checking our information on account of the inadequacy of the early accounts." Kennard, 1936, p. 2, has it: "The Mandans have lived among and intermarried with the Hidatsa to such an extent, that there are only three people alive today, both of whose parents spoke Mandan." Chafe's "fewer than 10 speakers" (1964) is inconclusive, since it derives from a crude questionnaire with which it is impossible to make finer distinctions (in Voegelin and Voegelin, 1964, p. 115). Bruner's opening sentence may also be pertinent (1961, p. 187): "The most striking fact about the Mandan is that they are 'extinct.'" Perhaps equally striking is the fact that monographs on this "extinct" people continue to be put forth purporting to reconstruct, with varying degrees of success, this hazy segment of culture history: Will and Spinden, 1906; Bowers, 1950 (but see Holder, 1950, for evaluation); Bruner, 1961; Wood, 1967; Holder, 1968.

[39] Henry, 1897, vol. 1, pp. 319–66; Lewis and Clark, 1904–1905, vol. 1, pp. 208–9; La Vérendrye, 1927, passim.

[40] La Vérendrye, 1927, p. 107.

belonged to the Fall Indians, subsequently identified as the Hidatsas and affiliated groups.[41] Some of the latter had come from horticultural pursuits along the Red River to the east, while others, from the north, seem to have had a more nomadic bent.[42]

The ethnic identification of the Mandans, and associated peoples, is no simple task. There are claims of movements from the east, the ultimate result of European maneuvers and the consequent restless wanderings of displaced native groups. This is in contrast to a more general long-term drift up the Missouri drainage system. Lewis and Clark, as well as Henry, learned at first hand that the Mandans had lived "on the Missourie low down" many years before. Because of local warfare they began to travel upstream until they came to the country of the Panias (Arikaras), where they lived as friends for many years until new warfare forced them upstream again to the

[41] Thompson, 1962, pp. 169, 172.

[42] Lewis and Clark, 1904–1905, vol. 1, p. 220, for Nov. 12, 1804 (omitted by Biddle); N.B. also idem, 1893, vol. 2, pp. 196–200, for Nov. 21, 1804 (an informative section offered by Biddle but missing in the original journals), and vol. 3, pp. 1176–77 (Coues's notes are helpful). Henry and Thompson, 1897, vol. 1, p. 322 and ff. (Coues is again helpful). In view of the importance of these first accurately located and described historic villages, it is surprising that archeological identification of them is difficult to come by and there is a paucity of archeological material and adequate observations from these specific settlements. Nevertheless, see Will and Spinden, 1906; Will, 1924; Will and Hecker, 1944. Bowers, 1965, pp. 10–25, 476–89, in a generally undocumented reconstruction makes no mention of specific archeological identification of these villages. Wood, 1967, also seems silent on the matter. Strong, 1940, pp. 362 ff., describes the Fort Abraham Lincoln site near Bismarck, N.D., as a "documented" but *unidentified* historic Mandan village of the mid-eighteenth century.

location visited by the explorers.⁴³ The precise number of Mandan villages is somewhat obscure—not more than thirteen, and as few as three in the various accounts, which may show internal inconsistencies. They never constituted a population comparable to the Arikaras with their thirty or forty villages scattered along the Missouri River in the first half of the eighteenth century.

Despite the ambiguities of this record the Mandans are clearly old residents of the Missouri Valley who early lived in horticultural villages. They conform in general to the pattern of the Plains horticulturalist, living in several economically autonomous earth-lodge villages located along the river terrace. At the hands of the women, the fields furnished the staple food supply with ample stored surplus, but there was also considerable dependence on wild game, brought in by the men. It is not clear that the Mandans regularly went on a communal bison hunt, although they told Thompson that they no longer went on extended group hunts because of enemy raids. The bison was important in their ceremonies, and elaborate animal-imitation dances called the bison nearer to the village. These ceremonies bore an erotic aspect, an element found in other rites of these people. Early observers comment on the "laxness" of the Mandans, by which, of course, they meant to cast aspersion on the women for their sexual freedom, found commonly in the Missouri River villages.⁴⁴

⁴³ Lewis and Clark, 1904–1905, vol. 1, p. 220. Henry, 1897, vol. 1, p. 334.

⁴⁴ Thompson, 1962, pp. 173, 176–78; Lewis and Clark, 1904–1905, vol. 1, pp. 244–45; idem, 1893, vol. 2, pp. 221–22 (Biddle elaborates); Henry and Thompson, 1897, vol. 1, pp. 326–27, 342, 348; Maximilian, 1906, vol. 23, pp. 324–34, and passim. Catlin, 1967, is a readily available reprinting of the original essay with

This would seem to indicate a relatively high status for women, comparable to that among the Arikaras. The matrilineal emphasis in Mandan life is even more marked. Descent was strictly reckoned in the female lines. There were well-defined matrilineal clans with exogamic rules. Lowie felt these may have developed from originally distinct villages. The clans evidently crosscut settlements, so that the Arikara tendency toward village endogamy did not apply.[45]

Dances and ceremonies extolling and imitating animals seem like the animal lodges of the Arikara shamans but lack a similar degree of organization and have little connection with curing.[46] The societies of the Mandans proliferated and were not confined to the men. Maximilian listed eight of these organizations, which differ from similar organizations among the Arikaras since they were age-graded.[47] They furnished a ladder by which the lowliest person could climb in status, given the requisite purchase prices. The same was true for the invention and sale of personal bundles by individuals, though less public acclaim would accrue from such a course. Descriptions of the transfer of so-called clan bundles seem contradictory. According to Bowers there was class division among the Mandans, reminiscent of the Arikara arrangement. Those in high status

helpful commentary by Ewers. Bowers, 1950, pp. 111–63, quotes much of Catlin and Maximilian, and adds traditional and hearsay accounts; caution in use is advised since he notes, p. ix, a "toning down of the accounts of the buffalo-calling rites with their sex licenses to make them readable without embarrassment to mixed audiences," reflecting an attitude which has long bedeviled Mandan ethnography.

[45] Bowers, 1950, pp. 118–20, 164–82.

[46] Lowie, 1913, pp. 294–323; 1916, pp. 942–46, and passim.

[47] Maximilian, 1906, vol. 23, pp. 324–34, which Bowers, 1950, reproduces verbatim in extenso, pp. 151–56; also Lowie, 1917.

were maintained in position by the ownership of clan bundles, but there was competitive buying and selling of the same bundles, not only among those of high status but also among the strivers. On the one hand a secure group was granted high status through access to supernatural sanctions, while on the other hand, their status could be purchased out from under them. The position of chief was strictly hereditary and descended from father to son. One wonders how the anomaly in inheritance was reconciled with the firm principle of reckoning descent in the female line, and just how the relation between the chieftainship and clan affiliation was determined.

The totality of Mandan society had a strong competitive tone. The many opportunities for the parvenu to raise himself are reminiscent of the "lower side" of Arikara society, with a proliferation of sodalities, war societies, dancing societies, personal bundles, purchase of clan bundles, and other such striving. The masochistic excesses of the Okipa ceremony, foreshadowing the sun dance in such impressive detail, would be more to the liking of the Boys' world than to that of the priests or even the shamans of the Arikara villages. Such priests as existed among the ancient Mandans did not hand down their lore to their latter-day successors in the same fashion as pertained among the Caddoan-speaking people. Nor for that matter do the shamans seem to have been able to muster their forces with the same élan as those of the Arikara and Pawnee villages.

The diverse origins of the Mandans may well account for the apparent lack of consistency in the above picture. This was compounded by the effects of increased enemy raiding, disease, attrition, and a dwindling away and realignment of villages, all characteristic of the eighteenth century, capped by the smallpox epidemic. Not only their upriver position but also the course of their historical development places these people at some remove from their linguistic relatives, the downstream sedentary Siouan-speaking villagers.

The Dhegiha Siouan groups afford even more insight into the nature of the late rivalries which affected the horticulturalists vis-à-vis both the Europeans and such mounted nomads as the Dakota Sioux. The Omahas and Poncas, and to a lesser extent the Kansas and Osages, were in a favorable position to intercept trade with the upriver settlements and thus seriously disrupt the economic life of the Caddoan-speaking villagers, increasingly dependent as they were on European goods.

The prehistory of the Dhegihan groups, especially the Omahas and Poncas, is incomplete. Most archeologists would derive the historic units from varieties of the Oneota archeological complex without much agreement as to the precise manner of development. The major features of the Oneota complex evidently represent reworkings and subsequent adaptations of influences coming from the main currents of cultural development to the eastward along the middle course of the Mississippi River. Recent work has led to claims of some eight centuries of cultural stability for the Oneota sequence in that area.[48] The pertinent Dhegihan derivations will surely be found in the seventeenth and eighteenth centuries. The whole complex seems to be distinct from the so-called Nebraska Culture materials found nearby along the Missouri River and bears no clear relation to manifestations northwest along the middle course of the stream. To the south, some authorities derive the historic Osages and Kansas directly from varieties of the

[48] Henning, 1967, p. 185.

74

Oneota complex.[49] Further research will clarify the origins of all these groups. A brief examination of their ethnology will show how they varied from the ideal example presented above.

These sedentary Siouan people all possessed a well-defined gentile and moiety system. In contrast to the ambiguity of clans for any Caddoan-speaking people, there is no doubt concerning unilateral descent groups among them. Although the gentes functioned primarily in relation to certain ceremonial prerogatives, they also defined rules of marriage. They appear to have cut across village organization. Sedentary villages of these Siouans apparently consisted of an endogamous cluster of gentes whose exogamous divisions and subdivisions could extend beyond village lines. Within the village, positions descended in the patrilineal family line and hereditary posts such as the priesthood were the prerogatives of specific gentes. The really important unit in the sedentary Siouan village was the patrilineal family. Even though patrilocality was the rule among the Omahas in the early nineteenth century, plural wives often accompanied their parents on communal hunts and the husband visited them in their own band encampment.[50]

Although the religion of these people is complex and shot through with horticultural elements, it is difficult to obtain a coherent and exact idea of the nature and function of their bundle system. The basic concept was present, but it does not appear to have been expanded to include true "tribal" or "village" bundles. The various bundles had both keepers and

[49] Wedel, 1959, pp. 57, 170–71, must be seen for a considered evaluation of such claims; also, Wedel, 1961, pp. 117–20.

[50] Fortune, 1932, pp. 13–17, 20; Fletcher and La Flesche, 1911, pp. 194–95; James, 1905, vol. 15, pp. 11–13; Dorsey, 1894.

the priests who manipulated them; the bundle secrets were learned through payments and those who learned the secrets became members in an organization of priests.[51] The Osage bundles were owned by specific gens members, but the bundle of one gens could be purchased by another gens and thus transferred. To treat an important tribal bundle in this way would hardly have suited the Caddoan speakers; the purchase of the knowledge was one thing, the removal or sale of the actual physical bundle was quite a different matter. From the Caddoan standpoint the Siouan system lacks the essential holiness and sacredness of the bundle and its associated religious system.

Similarly, while the basic concept of an original pure spirit or power is found, it is associated with the origin of the moiety and gentes. The ancestral gentile figures are said to have been embodied from this spirit into the forms of animals and objects which served as the "totems" of the gentes.[52] The fundamental dualism of Caddoan religion is found in both the moiety divisions and fertility concepts, but without astronomical elaborations such as those of the Pawnees. Early observers stated that the astronomical knowledge of the Osages was extremely limited. Much of the religious material is poorly recorded, but it seems evident that there was rather less formal organization of the theological system among these Siouans.[53]

The relative weakness of religious organization placed the Siouan chief in a somewhat anomalous position. He was certainly considered to be a more or less sacred figure. The basic dualism between life and death is found here, and both

[51] See, for example, Fletcher and La Flesche, 1911, pp. 62–63, 71 ff.

[52] Ibid., pp. 73, 134, 140–41; Dorsey, 1894.

[53] Nuttal, 1905, pp. 238–39; Tixier, 1940, p. 149. See the Introduction in Fortune, 1932.

the chief and the priest were prohibited from belonging to the same societies as the doctors. Yet the famous Blackbird rose to the position of chief of the Omahas by the overt use of in-group sorcery. At a time when the chieftainship of the Caddoan-speaking people was still sacred and inviolable, this sedentary Siouan chief is said to have resorted to the use of chemical poisons to maintain his position. Among the Osages there were also chiefs who possessed "curing powers."[54] When Pike visited the Osages in the early nineteenth century he remarked that although they possessed hereditary chiefs, there were many men who had, by their activity and boldness in war, more influence than those of illustrious ancestry. At a later date Nuttal noted that the regent, Clarmont, attempted to retain power after the rightful hereditary chief came of age. In the early literature there are suggestions that the power of the Omaha chiefs, once strong, was rapidly declining.[55]

The structuring of the doctors' association among the Omahas was not so complex as that of the Pawnees and Arikaras. There evidently were only four animal lodges and the inner divisions were not as elaborate. If anything, Omaha doctors were more open than their Caddoan counterparts in the use of sorcery, and their whole power was associated with the Midewiwin. This northern ceremony seems to be tightly integrated into the Omaha religion and magical system but is lacking among their Caddoan neighbors.[56]

The sedentary Siouans shared their basic agricultural techniques with the Caddoan speakers. Corn symbols appear in

[54] James, 1905, vol. 15, pp. 316 ff.; Fletcher and La Flesche, 1911, p. 82; La Flesche, 1914, p. 71.

[55] Pike, 1895, vol. 2, p. 626; Nuttal, 1905, pp. 237, 242; James, 1905, vol. 15, pp. 300, 316, 321.

[56] Fortune, 1932, pp. 25–26 ff.

their religious system, and planting and harvest rituals were important. Nevertheless, women do not appear to have occupied a high position in their social organization. Early observers remarked on the low status of the Siouan women.[57] Various attitudes of the Siouans toward their Caddoan neighbors are also revealing. Omaha traditions maintain that they learned both horticulture and the technique of earth-lodge construction from the Arikaras and that they were driven out of their original holdings along the Missouri River by the stronger Pawnees. A nineteenth-century Omaha anecdote is in character. An Omaha doctor visiting the Pawnees was challenged to duplicate a feat of the Pawnee doctors who were cutting off their tongues and replacing them. The Omaha accepted the challenge, cut off his tongue, and bled to death. Apocryphal or not, this story told by the Omahas themselves seems significant.[58] The Osages held the Wichitas in great awe as sorcerers who could control storms and cause men to lose their minds, although they frequently challenged the prior rights of these dangerous foes to the salines of eastern Kansas.[59]

In contrast to the Caddoan villagers, all these Siouans emphasized the chase at the expense of horticultural pursuits. There seems to be an implicit assumption among Plains specialists that the advent of the horse immediately increased hunting and turned interests away from horticultural life. It is held that the settled peoples increasingly leaned toward a hunting exist-

[57] James, 1905, vol. 15, pp. 22–23; Nuttal, 1905, p. 257; Tixier, 1940, pp. 170, 182.

[58] Fletcher and La Flesche, 1911, pp. 75 ff., 88; James, 1905, vol. 14, pp. 55–56.

[59] Tixier, 1940, pp. 155–86, 223–24, 230 (by "Pawnee" and "Pani Piquet," "Wichita" is intended); Forsyth in Blair, 1911, vol. 2, pp. 184, 198–99.

ence, to become really seminomadic by the middle of the nineteenth century. Nevertheless, among Caddoans the old, deeply rooted interest in and orientation toward the sanctity of horticulture in no way diminished, as witnessed by the details of their religious beliefs and their fundamental attitudes toward the horse.[60] These very people served as middlemen in the horse trade from the Spanish Southwest throughout the eighteenth century and later, because of old trade connections noted by Coronado in the sixteenth century. Their westerly location vis-à-vis the Siouans would in any case have given them easier access to the horse. Among the southern Caddos proper, horses are reported in considerable numbers by the late seventeenth century. At that time the Wichitas and the Pawnees were engaged in trade to the southwest, for branded horses and turquoise. By the end of the eighteenth century the Arikaras to the north had assumed their well-known nineteenth-century position as the main purveyors of horses along the middle stretches of the Missouri River. The Wichitas and Caddos in the south were serving the same function for such groups as the Osages.[61]

If the shift away from horticulture toward increased hunting was a simple matter of early access to the horse, it should be more marked among the Caddoans. Records from the eighteenth century show the opposite to be true. To the European traders the Caddoans seemed more interested in farming. The sedentary Siouans could be relied upon to serve only as hunters,

[60] Weltfish, 1965, pp. 140–43.

[61] Joutel, in Margry, 1876–88, vol. 3, pp. 338, 347, 423; Tonti, in Kellogg, 1917, pp. 316–17, 321; Deliette in De Gannes, 1934, pp. 388–89; Trudeau, 1914, pp. 472–74; Bolton, 1914, pp. 167–68, 321; Haines, 1938b; Ewers, 1955, pp. 2–15. Roe, 1955, must also be consulted in extenso.

Tribe	Distance from St. Louis	Occupation	Number of Warriors	Enemies
Little Osage	85	Hunters and horse-stealers	350–500	All Mississippi tribes
Cances (Kansas)	150	Hunters, some agriculture	350	Panis, and La Republica (Pawnees)
La Republica (Republican Pawnee)	250 on the Cances (Republican) River, 110 from the Missouri	Hunting and agriculture	350–400	Cances and Big Osages
Panis (Pawnee)	250 on branch of Platte River	Gives considerable time to cultivation of maize ... can be easily reduced to the cultivation of any other product	500–600	Cances and the Sioux
Majas (Omaha)	280. On a small tributary of the Misuri about 80 leagues from the mouth of the Platte	Hunters but have enough agriculture for their own needs	400–500	Cances
Big Osages	180. On banks of a river emptying into the Missouri of about 140 leagues in length	Hunters and horse-stealers	800	La Republica, Panis, Piquies (Wichitas), Hotos Alkanos (Arkansas), and the tribes living on the Mississippi in English territory

but the Pawnees could raise enough food to support trading establishments at their villages. Much the same, of course, held true for the Arikaras. A report compiled in 1777 by the Spanish authorities in Louisiana gives some significant information.[62]

Despite lacunae this table suggests less horticultural specialization for the sedentary Siouans. Perhaps these people represent hunting-and-gathering groups who came into their area of historical occupancy relatively late and never completely assimilated the horticultural way of life. Their traditions of a late northeastern origin support this speculation. The similarity of their disparate dialects was noted by the early explorers and interpreted as evidence of their recent geographic expansion. However, and whenever, they came into their geographical positions, they were ideally situated to become the rivals of the Caddoans for the increasing European trade pushing westward from the Mississippi Valley after the end of the seventeenth century.[63]

With the acquisition of the Louisiana Territory in 1763, Spain continued to expand the trade methods of the French. However, instead of trusting the exploitation of the fur resources to individual operators working out from fortified centers along the Mississippi, Spain decided to make the fur trade go hand in hand with her military policy of establishing a Missouri River buffer against the British in Canada. Expeditions began to push up that river. To the native populations the new situation meant that trade goods would be available in increasing amounts. Siouan villagers on the easternmost fringes of the Plains could now dominate trade destined for the west.

[62] See table page 80. Modified from Houck, 1909, vol. 1, pp. 141–46.

[63] James, 1905, vol. 15, pp. 130–32, 135, 136; Pike, 1895, vol. 2, p. 525; Bradbury, 1904, p. 80.

Thus there arose a new commercial basis for conflict. The fur interests wished to reach the Caddoan villages and establish posts, and the Caddoans were anxious to remain middlemen and to siphon off trade goods, but there was always the danger that the Siouans would intercept the shipments. The tense situation was not ameliorated by the increasing appearance of displaced Indians from the eastern seaboard pressing westward against the Siouans, nor did the increasing acceptance of the horse by new groups moving out into the Plains make conditions easier.

The economic blockade is well documented. In the north the Omahas and Poncas jeopardized traders' efforts to ascend the upper Missouri River. These two tribes did not necessarily cooperate; traders who were successful in passing the Omahas might well be raided farther up the river by the Poncas. Blackbird, chief of the Omahas, gave MacKay, the Spanish representative, assurance that he would prevent the Poncas from bothering the expeditions, but he could not possibly enforce such an order. Aware of the Anglo-Spanish rivalry, Blackbird used the implied threat of shifting his support to the English to bargain better with MacKay. As a final measure he made the grandiose gesture of offering to "send the pipe" to the nomadic Dakota Sioux who held the territory between the Poncas and the Arikaras, although it was impossible for an Omaha chief, however powerful, to control the Dakotas. Furthermore, it was not the nomads who were the real threat to upriver traffic but precisely the horticulturalists with whom MacKay was attempting to drive a bargain. Regarding the danger presented by the nomadic Dakota Sioux, Trudeau said,

There is little risk of meeting the Sioux. They are easily evaded by proper precaution in passing the places where they frequent. Above all it is necessary to know how to choose the time to make the passage when they are away, which is in the early spring.[64]

To the south, in the central reaches of the Plains, along the southerly affluents of the Missouri River, the Kansas played much the same role. The Spanish authorities in Saint Louis noted that the Kansas were uniformly hostile to the tribes of the Missouri River, specifically the Republican band of Pawnees; because of this they made trouble for any traders sent to the Pawnees. Furthermore, they did not allow expeditions up the river, their aim being to prevent arms and ammunition from reaching the western groups.[65] Some years later Lewis and Clark faced the same problem on their return journey:

This being part of the Missouri the Kansaz nation resort to at this season of the year for the purpose of robbing the perogues passing up to other nations above, we have every reason to expect to meet with them, and agreeably with their common custom of examining every thing in the perogues and takeing what they want out of them, it is probable that they may wish to take those liberties with us.[66]

Along the lower course of the Arkansas River the Osages were playing much the same game. They shared Omaha-Ponca attitudes regarding the passage of goods bound upstream for the Wichitas. Not only did they oppose the Europeans, but they were also on a war footing against the Caddoans, a condition mentioned by Tonti as early as 1690. Consciously or not, the Osages were serving as a native catspaw for the English, a role

[64] Houck, 1909, vol. 2, pp. 187–89; Trudeau, 1914, pp. 463–64.
[65] Houck, 1909, vol. 1, p. 143.
[66] Lewis and Clark, 1904–1905, vol. 5, p. 384, Sept. 14, 1806.

clearly evaluated by the Spaniards in 1777 when they planned a military campaign to destroy an Osage village mounting some eight hundred warriors. The Spaniards were also anxious to utilize the Skiri Pawnees, who then had some six hundred to eight hundred warriors available near the Wichitas. The Skiris were interested in aiding the colonial powers against their ancient enemy, the Osages. Their recent migration had been motivated by thoughts of joining with their Texas relatives under Spanish aegis. In 1786 the Spaniards succeeded in bringing about a treaty between the Osages and the Caddos, but later the same year the Osage broke the treaty by attacking the Caddos and the Kitsais and running off bands of their horses.[67]

Despite blockades and complications, trading was established with both the Caddoan-speaking people and their Siouan rivals. The horticultural villages were ideal bases of operation for the European entrepreneurs by the very nature of their stability. Although there were obvious advantages to the native people as a result of the trade goods which passed through their villages, the ultimate disadvantages were greater. The most immediate danger brought by the newcomers were epidemics of new diseases which swept across the villages; measles, small-pox, and venereal infections found ideal hosts in the villages. The very nature of life there meant that the mildest infection could rapidly become epidemic. On the other hand, the rising equestrian nomads, thanks to their loosely organized and shifting population units, stood to suffer smaller losses. The effects of depopulation from disease must have contributed greatly to the decline of the horticulturalists.

[67] Tonti, in Kellogg, 1917, p. 315; Bolton, 1914, vol. 2, pp. 122, 141, 145; Houck, 1909, vol. 2, pp. 253 ff.

Archeological research has shown that the villages of the early and middle eighteenth century were generally small hamlets containing twenty to forty or so lodges. Historical and ethnographic accounts allow us to assume that about fifteen people inhabited each lodge. Thus the thirty-two populous villages of the Arikaras in the ancient times reported by J. B. Trudeau must have represented a population of considerably more than fifteen thousand. By the 1790s, he continues, several sieges of smallpox had nearly destroyed them, sparing only a few families from any village. Trudeau himself visited the two large villages into which the scattered hamlets were consolidated briefly near the confluence of the Cheyenne with the Missouri River. The two large and one briefly occupied smaller village, above the confluence of the Grand and the Missouri River, were occupied for some thirty years at the beginning of the nineteenth century. Lewis and Clark reported that the smallest village had sixty lodges. Archeological and other historical reports indicate a figure of considerably more occupied lodges in each of the other villages. Pierre Antoine Tabeau, the resident trader, estimated about five hundred men able to bear arms. This compares favorably with Trudeau's figure for the earlier villages at the Cheyenne River, whereas the Arikaras were formerly able to muster some four thousand men. Allowing for exaggeration and inaccuracies, there is little doubt that there had been a very real reduction and consolidation due not only to disease but, as Lewis and Clark put it, the "Commotion and war with their neighbors," by which they had been "reduced and compelled to come together for protection."[68]

[68] Trudeau, 1914, pp. 459–61; Tabeau, 1939, pp. 123–24; Lewis and Clark, 1904–1905, vol. 1, p. 188 (not in Biddle).

Furthermore, the Plains were rapidly filling with fully nomadic hunters. The Cheyennes had moved across the Missouri and become equestrian, followed shortly by the Dakota Sioux groups. Native warfare affecting the Missouri River villages throughout the eighteenth century was apparently intensified at the very time the Europeans were becoming established there. Whatever character the warfare assumed later in the nineteenth century, at this period it appears to have been deadly and serious.

As the population of a village declined to the point of disintegration, the old way of life was not abandoned. The solution was that of combining the remnants of originally autonomous villages into a single village. The combination was awkward since the old loyalties continued in the new situation and there was increasing tension within the social structure of the villages. Schisms appeared and the old stable authority of the leading families was threatened. Nevertheless, this authority was never lost. To the very last the status structuring of the villages remained, although the leaders often found themselves powerless to control raiding parties, just at the period when the wild and irresponsible behavior of raiders could do serious damage as the contacts between groups proliferated. In this setting alliances with out-groups were brittle, and within the village itself strains appeared in the old social structure.

The distribution of a new form of wealth, the horse, may have constituted a problem for some time, and any stresses became even more acute with the success of the surrounding nomads who gave ample precept for the strivers. A new pattern of life had appeared on the Plains; as the cultural revolution matured it was proving eminently successful. Hunting groups and casual gardeners found the new pattern easy to accept and were streaming onto the Plains in increasing numbers.

The old ways of the horticulturalists did not go under easily. Resistance to sudden change was deeply ingrained in the whole village fabric. We have seen much of the patterning which led inevitably to this resistance. We can now consider the relations between the horticulturalists and the equestrian nomads in more detail, not only to see how and why the nomads were successful but also to better understand why the horticulturalists were never, so to speak, successful in making the shift to nomadism.

The Villages Face Nomadism

In the New World, as elsewhere, subsistence by hunting and gathering to the exclusion of cultivation long preceded the latter. Hunting practices associated with herds of grazing animals on the Plains have an antiquity of at least twelve thousand years. The entrapping of bison at specially selected sites in some parts of the northwestern Plains goes back some four thousand years.[1] These traditions of hunting on foot have no direct continuity with the wanderers reported from the

[1] Wedel, 1961, pp. 46–86, summarizes the scattered sources; Willey, 1966, pp. 313–17, gives a condensed and differing version; Frison, 1967, reports prehistoric bison hunting with continuity to historic groups.

southern Plains in the sixteenth century, nor do the latter have a demonstrable connection with the mounted hunters of historic times.

The first Spanish explorers moving northeastward from Mexico met groups of nomads on foot far out on the Plains. These hunters and gatherers had close trade relations with horticultural groups, not only those of the Rio Grande but also along the large rivers to the east. Their eastern markets were the villages of the Caddoan-speaking horticulturalists.[2] Much the same relations pertained two hundred years later regarding the equestrian nomads, although the best explanation for the rapid growth of these groups of mounted hunters is to derive them from areas outside the Plains proper.[3] By the nineteenth century the Plains west of the horticulturalists were filled with linguistically diverse equestrian nomads who ranged over enormous areas. Along the eastern fringe of the Plains the horticultural bloc was interrupted: the Arikaras were separated from the Omaha-Poncas and the Pawnees by the Dakota Sioux. Just west of the Dakotas another group of nomads, the Cheyennes, were mid-stride in a shift from marginal horticulture to equestrian nomadism at the time of our first records.

The Cheyennes were a small group of Algonquian-speaking people who strayed far southwesterly from their cogeners about the Great Lakes. The fame of their military exploits and bitter experiences during the last three quarters of the nineteenth century has grown out of all proportion to their size as a tribal entity. They appear only briefly in the theater of culture

[2] Castañeda's account of 1540 explorations in Hammond and Ray, 1940, see pp. 235–36, 260–61. See also Winship, 1896.

[3] Wissler, 1906, long ago made this point, supported by Kroeber, 1939, and reiterated over the years by later workers, e.g., Oliver, 1962.

change along the Missouri River. They display in capsule form one kind of variation that can be played on the simple theme of the shift from a sedentary to a nomadic way of life. Within less than three generations they abandoned their earth-lodge villages along the Sheyenne River in the Red River drainage system and by the end of the eighteenth century had briefly joined the Arikara villages near the Grand-Missouri confluence. They left their gardens permanently within a decade or so to move into the Black Hills of South Dakota, which again they abandoned by the late 1830s. They long retained ties of friendship with the Arikaras and developed a widespread trade which brought them to the annual Missouri River trade fairs for many years after they had moved even farther southwest into what is today eastern Wyoming and Colorado. During this short time they had completely forsaken horticultural pursuits, had become well-known traffickers, and had adopted the way of life of the mounted hunters of the plains in all its minutiae.[4] Since their course of development took them on westward, they played no large role in the conflicts that developed along the Missouri River proper. Their struggles lay in the arena of conflict between the successful horse nomads and the encroaching United States forces, military and otherwise.

The Cheyennes withdrew from the country about Lake Superior under pressure from such neighboring groups as the Assiniboins. Presumably they later left their earth-lodge villages along the Sheyenne River because of the activities of the Dakota Sioux, who were in conflict with groups of Ojibways.

[4] Tabeau, 1939, pp. 151–52; Henry and Thompson, 1897, vol. 1, pp. 144–45; Mooney, 1905–1907, pp. 363–68; Grinnell, 1923, vol. 1, pp. 1–46; Swanton, 1930; Strong, 1940, pp. 370–75; Jablow, 1951, pp. 1–10; Lewis and Clark, 1893, vol. 1, pp. 146–49 and footnotes (not in Lewis and Clark, 1904–1905, same entry date).

Thus the movement of the Cheyennes is another ultimate result of the displacement of native peoples in the east and in the final analysis a result of European intrusions into North America. The Cheyennes did not move as a tribal unit. The tribal unity noted for these people in the nineteenth century is probably again a late manifestation resulting from the conflicts encountered during their life on the Plains. The move from the Sheyenne River villages to the Missouri was made at widely separated times by different groups of Cheyennes. While there were still semihorticultural villages of these people along the Missouri, where they were friends with the Arikaras and Mandans, other groups of the same people had migrated farther to the west, where they had already abandoned horticultural pursuits and now traded into the Missouri River villages as specialized hunters. At that time, during the first three decades of the nineteenth century, groups of Cheyennes were scattered all the way from the vicinity of the Arikara villages on the Missouri River to the upper course of the Arkansas River far to the southwest. They had also spread to the north along the lower course of the Little Missouri River, and were trading with the Mandans. The eighteenth-century Spanish settlements in the far Southwest had already seen Cheyenne groups long before these final movements. During the first few decades of the nineteenth century the Black Hills of western South Dakota were the center of the range of all these peoples. By mid-century that area had become the country of the western groups of Dakotas.

Not only was there diversity in the movement of the Cheyenne, but this was also true for their tribal unity. The first of them to reach the Black Hills found there a related group called the Suhtais. These people spoke a closely related dialect and had migrated from the Minnesota country many years before. The Suhtais joined the Cheyennes and became an integral part of the tribe throughout the remainder of the nine-teenth century. Furthermore, the move onto the Plains was followed shortly by a tacit division of the whole group into southern and northern branches, a division which seems to have been mainly geographical, and only later had any political or tribal meaning.

Once they were on the open plains and dependent on the bison herds, their political organization and settlement pattern took on a form characteristic of nomadic groups.[5] Despite an overall tribal organization which involved a council of forty-four chiefs, the whole people seldom had an opportunity to come together except at times of annual ceremonial activities. Grinnell tells us that for the most part the people were divided into small self-sufficient groups whose main concern was getting food sufficient to carry on from day to day. These encampments were scattered over the bison country, moving about in keeping with the demands of hunting, sometimes joining with another such camp, often losing families or mem-bers who might wander off to join with others for a visit or even to seek common cause with the new group on a permanent basis. Frequently in good season two or more groups combined their forces, remaining together for many months, only to disperse later and go their separate ways. A running report and flow of news concerning the location and fortunes of the various groups passed about. Such news was especially important when large numbers were able to come together in observance of

[5] Eggan, 1937, pp. 33–95, and again in 1955, pp. 48–55, also 1952, 1966, pp. 45–77, presents a "reconstruction" mainly on the basis of kinship terminologies.

ceremonies. Thus a tribal identity was maintained even with such scattering of the actual people. If we add the increasing problems of military necessities, the Cheyennes as fully equestrian nomadic bison hunters, raiders, and traders present quite a different configuration from the Arikaras and Mandans in the villages which the Cheyennes had forsaken.

Yet the details of the beliefs and customs of the Cheyennes bear unmistakable witness to their former sedentary horticultural way of life. Despite the exigencies of nomadic life the position of women in the scheme of things was considerably higher than among the Dakotas, more reminiscent of that among the Arikaras and Mandans. According to Grinnell, descent was weighted in the female line. Membership in the tribal division, or named band, was determined along lines of descent through females. Residence of the newly married couples was said to be with the band of the wife and her female relatives, although by the end of the nineteenth century these rules were in abeyance and young people felt that descent should be reckoned through the male line. Those were reservation times and the old way of life was nearly gone. In the days of initial ethnographic study there was some feeling among the older people that the bands had once been groups of kindred with rules of exogamy, that is to say, clans with matrilineal descent. As late as 1900 the old people felt that the bands were composed of kindred, the descendants of a common ancestor. Eggan, on the basis of a review of available ethnographic reports, said:

The feeling concerning descent is bilateral, or even slightly patrilineal at present, but matrilocal residence led to the identification of children with the mother's band, for the most part. Each band was composed of a group of extended households based on matri-local residence, and as such was a self-sufficient economic unit.[6]

Professor Hoebel's brief sketch of Cheyenne life denies the matrilineal emphasis noted by Grinnell's older informants and dismisses the evidence out of hand as "hardly convincing." [7] The matter seems somewhat more complex than this brief comment would indicate. It is likely that the matrilineal weighting was a real factor remaining as a fragment of the old horti-cultural ways long after other aspects had gone. Grinnell, our greatest authority, states that:

The women are the rulers of the camp. They act as a spur to the men, if they are slow in performing their duties. They are far more conservative than the men, and often hold them back from hasty, ill-advised action. If the sentiment of the women of the camp clearly points to a certain course as desirable, the men are quite sure to act as the women wish.[8]

There was explicit ranking among Cheyenne families. A good family depended on brave men and good, industrious women. Also it should possess "more or less property." The chiefly ideals presented by Grinnell are virtually identical with those of the Arikaras. There were said to be forty-four chiefs for the whole tribe, but there were only four leading chiefs— one for each constituent band. Furthermore, these latter were men of special importance and influence. The forty subchiefs might better be thought of as councilors, their opinions being on a par with those of war chiefs and heads of the soldier

[6] Eggan, 1937, p. 37, also 1955; Grinnell, 1923, has the basic data.

[7] Hoebel, 1960, p. 22.

[8] Grinnell, 1923, vol. 1, pp. 128–29.

societies. The opinions of the head chiefs counted. Since they were allowed to name their successors, capable sons tended to replace their fathers. Grinnell felt that these offices were hereditary.

Hoebel's sketch emphasizes the dichotomy between the peace and the war functions of the chief. He was mainly concerned with peaceful activities. A leading chief must forswear the post of war chief or membership in soldier societies. The division between peace and war activities is reminiscent of the situation in the horticultural villages and the southeast generally. It accords well with the personality ideal sketched in by Grinnell. Hoebel's account also speaks of "the head priest-chief of the tribe," who is nowhere described in any detail. He is called the Sweet Medicine Chief and by virtue of his offices is in possession of the Sweet Medicine Bundle, a talisman passed on with the office. Grinnell maintains silence concerning such details, but according to Hoebel's impressionistic sketch the Sacred Arrow Bundle has many characteristics in common with the tribal bundles of the village peoples. It is "the embodiment of the tribal soul." An Arikara would be unlikely to so describe the village bundle but its purpose was the same. The life of the tribe depended on the existence of the bundle.

Serious crimes within the community called for a renewal ceremony in which, at the time of the summer solstice, the bundle was unwrapped and purified. There was not only an officiating bundle priest but also a bundle keeper. The ceremony brought the whole tribe together. Many of these details are reminiscent of the village-bundle complex. Their tenacity despite the vicissitudes of nomadic life is remarkable. Great secrecy surrounds the details of the beliefs. Perhaps a full account of the complex will someday reveal even more remnants of the old village way of life.[9]

These people did not abruptly leave the sedentary life, nor did they immediately cut themselves off from the Missouri River villages. Early nineteenth-century accounts mention regular trade fairs at which the Cheyennes met with the Arikaras or, to the north, with the Mandans. These fairs were held both in the villages and to the west along the escarpment of the Black Hills. They were considerable affairs at which horses and products of the chase were exchanged for garden produce and European trade goods.[10] Not only had the Cheyennes spent some time settled near the Arikaras, but further upstream they retained close if intermittent contact with them. The history of their relations reveals little warfare between these new nomads and their old sedentary friends, but the Dakota Siouan groups present a different picture.

The western groups of Dakotas from the earliest times are reported as raiding not only the Missouri River villagers, but also the European trading expeditions. Once the Missouri River was crossed they became the main enemy of all villagers. They originally occupied country north and east of the Missouri River as far as the Great Lakes. This area can be divided conveniently into the easterly wooded lake country and the westerly fringes of the grasslands between the Mississippi River affluents and the Missouri River. The French of the late seventeenth century clearly distinguish between the Sioux of the East and Sioux of the West, or the Woods and the Prairie Sioux. The Sioux of the Woods seem to have continued a

[9] Stands in Timber and Liberty, 1967, pp. 73–91, gives added detail on this and the Sacred Hat Bundle.
[10] Jablow, 1951, considers this in some detail.

woodland-hunting existence in Minnesota far into the nine-teenth century. The Sioux of the Prairie, which may have furnished the group later known as Tetons and Yanktons, are from the earliest times placed on the prairies. As early as the mid-seventeenth century these peoples were hunters living in skin tents and practicing a minimum of horticulture. Perrot indicates that their contact with the Panys (Pawnees) before this time had brought them the calumet ceremony. By 1766 the western groups were nomadic hunters in the prairie Plains. They lived in tents and wandered to the west, where they came into contact with hostile equestrian nomads from whom they protected themselves by retreating into patches of woods or swampy land.[11]

The initial displacement of native groups under Iroquois pressure seems to have forced these people away from the Great Lakes. Throughout most of the eighteenth century conflict with the Ojibways forced them farther southwest toward the Missouri. In the early 1740s they were embroiled with the Assiniboins and were raiding and ambushing along the trails from Rainy Lake to the Mandan villages. By 1774 even the Yanktons had adopted the horse. The exact time at which the Dakotas first crossed the Missouri remains to be established. By 1790 the Mandans were reportedly perpetually at war with them. In 1793–95 they were threatening Spanish trading expeditions in the neighborhood of the Poncas and Arikaras. They were also along the river some eighty leagues above the Omahas at odds with the Arikaras. Their occupation of the

[11] Blair, 1911, vol. 1, pp. 159–63, 170, 186, 245, 277; vol. 2, pp. 112–29. Margry, vol. 1, pp. 53–55; vol. 6, pp. 15, 22–23, 38, 56, 69–87, 534, 541, 556–60, 576, 610, 636–52. Carver, 1779, pp. 46, 60, 75, 221, 243, 278, 280. Landes, 1968, adds details.

north (east) bank of the Missouri was seasonal. They retained old trade ties with the British and withdrew northward periodically for European goods. In 1797 they were again attacking the Mandans. In all of this coming and going there was a drift toward the southwest. Some of these peoples remained along the easterly fringes and never did become dwellers on the open Plains. The westerly bands, however, rapidly adopted the life of equestrian nomads, and became thoroughly alienated from the old way of life. Thus the Dakota Sioux were a culturally heterogeneous people having a long history of contact with European influences.[12]

The Dakotas should be seen as a widespread group of people speaking closely related dialects of a common tongue, but being distinguished among themselves mainly on the basis of their geographical location. There have always been large named groups among the Dakotas, but these names vary with the period. The composition of the constituent groups clearly was not stable. There was a plethora of names but none of them were stable tribal designations. Nevertheless, there were certain stabilities with regard to geographical location, especially after the beginning of the nineteenth century.

The Teton Dakotas crossed the Missouri and occupied increasing areas of the country to the west and south, ultimately reaching the mountains and the high Plains country south of the Black Hills and west of the 100th meridian. Seven bands composed the nineteenth-century Teton Division: Brule, Minneconjou, Blackfeet, Two Kettles, Sans Arcs, Hunkpapa, and Oglala; information concerning the latter is by far the best.

[12] Henry, 1921, pp. 189, 195–96, 232. La Vérendrye, 1927, pp. 380, 430–31. Pond, 1933, pp. 58–59. Nasatir, 1927, p. 58; 1929–30, pp. 373, 511. Trudeau, 1914, 463–64. Thompson, 1962, p. 214.

Denig, the observant fur trader, reported on the basis of first-hand knowledge that by the fourth decade of the nineteenth century the Teton Dakotas alone had some 1,630 lodges, which he judged would give them a population of about 8,000. The bands of the Yanktons at that time amounted to only some 3,600 people. The bands of the Tetons had occupied the country west of the Missouri. The Brules ranged from the mid-course of the White River northward to the headwaters of the Little Missouri and the Bad River, on westward to the Badlands. The Oglalas, basing themselves in the south on the Platte about Fort Laramie, ranged to the north across the Black Hills as far as the headwaters of the Bad River, extended down the Cheyenne to its mid-course, and also frequented the country about the head of the Grand River. During the summer bands of young men raided far south into the valleys of the Platte and the Arkansas. These raids were for horses, and the raiders frequently returned from a single expedition with as many as fifty or sixty head. Pawnee settlements were raided en route.

The Minneconjous ranged along the Missouri between the Cheyenne River and the lower course of the Grand. The small Two Kettles band occupied the country south of the Grand to the Cheyenne River. Together with the Sans Arcs and the Blackfeet, the Hunkpapas occupied the country along the Moreau, Cannonball, and Heart rivers as well as the lower course of the Grand. According to Denig the bands were so mixed as to be scarcely distinguishable. They were alternately at war and peace with the Arikaras, Mandans, and Hidatsas. By the time the Arikaras had occupied the former Mandan villages at Fort Clark, Dakota bands were carrying on a considerable trade with them, exchanging skins, furs, meats, etc., for their corn and other garden produce. Since the summers were filled with pursuit of the bison herds and the stealing of horses, this trade normally was heaviest in the fall, and frequently continued into the winter, when it became more akin to begging.[13]

The record along the Missouri begins with Trudeau's observations of the 1790s concerning wandering bands of Dakotas along both sides of the Missouri and continues through the accounts of the Saone bands living with or near the Arikaras at the time of the Lewis and Clark exploration. It increases in volume and accuracy through the middle of the nineteenth century to the Battle of the Little Big Horn and the Ghost Dance uprisings in the closing decades of the century. Yet despite the abundant and revealing records there is still no major monograph to which one can turn for a picture of these people. There is nothing comparable to Grinnell's work on the Cheyennes or Lowie's sequence of studies of the Crows. Nevertheless, the picture of the western Dakota bands which emerges from the scattered references is consistent and in such contrast to that of the surrounding peoples that it is possible to present a sketch which will characterize them and also illuminate their mortal struggle with the horticultural villagers.

It is difficult to give a simple and general characterization of all these Dakota Sioux groups. They all possessed a remarkably resilient social structure, whose easy contours have been characterized as "anarchistic" by some observers. These groups all were able to change their social and political fealties with remarkable ease. There was no Sioux Nation, although the Europeans tried assiduously to so characterize these groups. They were little better than loose aggregates of more or less closely related family groups. The constituent families were

[13] Denig, 1961, pp. 14–29 and passim.

held together through the male line and their continuance depended to a great degree on the exploits and adventures of the men. The importance of these lines in the maintenance of leadership is pinpointed in the observations of Parkman among the Oglalas:

Bull Bear's son aspires to emulate his father's power. His chance is good, for besides his bravery and resolute character, he has more than 30 brothers. Henry [Parkman's companion], his brother-in-law, is told that he need fear nothing, for nobody will dare to touch him, since he has so many relations growing up around him. Family connections are evidently a great source of power.[14]

Such family lines might come together in large or small aggregates for common cause during greater or shorter periods of time, depending on the issues at hand. Leading men appeared who, in council with other leading heads of family lines, could give tone to the entire aggregate and in no small measure determine the direction of overall activities of the group. The continuance of their direction was dependent on the success of the operations. The position of seeming authority also was dependent on lavish giving by the head men. This is another version of the gift-giving practice which we have seen under different guise among the Arikaras. A strong leader of one season might through a series of reverses become a mere follower in a completely different band within the passage of a year. Furthermore, his whole "family" might well follow him in the peregrination.

Denig, writing in the 1850s after some thirty years of intimate experience with these people, has interesting opinions concern-

[14] Parkman, 1947, vol. 2, p. 446, June 23, 1846; Eggan, 1937, 1955, and Hassick, 1944, discuss the kinship system.

ing the attitude which any group of Tetons might have toward the traders and other intruders into the country. He concurs in general with other observers concerning the violence and self-destructiveness of individuals. He tells in detail of the death of a leading man, La Corne Seule. This man lost his favorite wife to sickness. Overcome with grief, he declared that he was going to throw away his life. Thereafter he sought out and wounded a bull bison. On foot and armed only with a knife, he then attacked it to the death. He was no match for the horns of the animal and was promptly gored to death, being later found on the prairie by a search party. Parkman has much to say concerning suicidal acts among the Oglalas of his day. His laconic journal brings the whole matter into sharp focus:

. . . that species of desperation in which an Indian upon whom fortune frowns resolves to throw away his body, rushing desperately upon any danger that offers. If he comes off successful he gains great honor. To show his bravery, an Indian rushed up to a grizzly bear and struck him three times on the head with his bow. Such acts are common.[15]

Denig points out that the group attitude toward the outside world was to a great extent determined by the individual character of the man who chanced to be their leader. It was the leading man who ultimately determined the object on which the violence of his individual followers would focus. Since the leadership might change with the fortunes and accidents of this man, and ultimately were dependent on his ability to give largesse, the attitudes of the various groups would seem to shift with the wind and follow an unpredictable course. A reasonable

[15] Denig, 1961, pp. 23–24; Parkman, 1947, vol. 2, p. 446.

and wise leader would appear to have wise followers; if a wild and irresponsible one succeeded him, the nature of the whole group was likely to correspond.

The occupation of the Plains west of the Missouri and the flowering there of the equestrian Dakotas did not ease their pressure on the Missouri horticulturalists. They were still interrupting trade bound for the Arikaras and Mandans in 1811 when the Astorians came upstream. In 1823 the Yanktons and Teton Dakotas joined the United States punitive expedition under Colonel Henry Leavenworth and attacked the Arikaras.[16] This warfare could hardly be considered as merely a game. It had serious disruptive effects on the way of life of the horti- culturalists. A report from the fur trader Denig may give the flavor of the conflict. In 1835 some Arikara Boys together with Pawnee raided along the L'Eau Qui Court River and captured forty or fifty horses from the encampment of some wandering Dakotas. The Dakotas tracked them down, recovered the horses, and killed twenty-two raiders. The warriors then re- turned to camp with the heads, hands, feet, and other parts of the dead. The hands and feet were paraded through the camp, impaled on sticks. Cords were attached to the scalped heads, then they were dragged about in the dirt, pelted with stones, beaten with sticks and shot at with arrows by small boys. The old women of the camp entered into the spirit of the occasion and encouraged the total destruction of the war mementos.[17] It must have been this constant threat and example of the highly successful Dakota equestrian nomads which led remnants of the old Arikara villages to try a few years of nomadic existence

[16] Bradbury, 1904, p. 103; Chittenden, 1935, vol. 2, pp. 589, 601; Dale, 1941, p. 75.
[17] Denig, 1961, p. 18.

before they returned to the Missouri in the late 1830s and took up residence with the Mandans and Hidatsas, once again attempting the horticultural solution.

In the historical accounts of the horticultural peoples the Dakotas are an almost classically stylized enemy figure. These people were one of the most successful representatives of the new way of life. Their transition from nomadic hunting afoot to full equestrian patterns was amazingly rapid. The whole change seems to have taken place in two generations. But it was merely the end phase of a long process which had been maturing for more than a century. The Dakotas had played the part of producers in the fur trade with Europeans since the last half of the seventeenth century. The groups described by Jonathan Carver and Peter Pond after the mid-eighteenth century were not untouched savages; they had some one hundred years of familiarity with European cultural elements. Nevertheless, the level of native socio-economic development was never much more than that of hunting and gathering. There was only a lapse of some twenty-five to thirty years between their access to the horse and the time when they became horsemen. There seems to have been about twenty-five years between their full adaptation to the horse and their appearance in numbers along the Missouri.

Fortunately, an acute and articulate observer, Pierre Antoine Tabeau, spent considerable time among the western bands of Dakotas along the Missouri River from 1802 through the winter of 1803/1804. His observations are keen, his comments are trenchant. He caught the Tetons when they were challenging all comers along the Missouri River. There were four thousand men bearing arms among the Dakotas. With the exception of the two small groups still near the Saint Peters

River far to the north, they were all migratory. They followed the herds of bison over the prairies to the north and east of the Missouri River, returning in the winter to camp along the sheltered bottoms or to hang about the villages of the horti-culturalists. Tabeau too comments on the resilience of the social organization which allowed these Siouan groups to expand at such a rapid rate. He describes the individual com-petition which grew out of the old northern woodland hunting tradition of individual status mobility and effloresced in the rapidly expanding economy of the horse nomads. The various tribes, particularly the Tetons, were subdivided under sub-ordinate chiefs who returned to the rank of "mere companions" when all were assembled together. The mode of living forced the people into small groups among which many feuds and petty jealousies arose.

This proclivity to quarrel was especially pronounced among the multitude of chiefs or leading men. Thus he says, "By a just defiance, which experience sanctions, a Teton is always armed, even in his lodge." Furthermore, the authority of the so-called chiefs was severely limited, and was "as naught before the opposition of a simple soldier." [18] He continues with a detailed account of a "mere soldier" who effectively held up the passage of one of his boats. Although there could have been collusion between the chief and the soldier in this instance, the many observations of petty thefts and jealousies show the individual to be supreme in Dakota society.

Violence and willful behavior were the order of the day among those vested with authority. At the trader's temporary store, a native guard was set. However, a Boy, defying the guard, climbed the roof and peeped in between the loosely set

[18] Tabeau, 1939; the material is culled from pp. 101–17 and ff.

planks. The soldier, tipping the ball from his revolver, fired directly through the crack. The Boy, blinded and bloody, tumbled from his perch and made his way back to his own lodge. There were no complaints; this was the prerogative of the soldiers in such duty. But vengefulness remained. The next evening under cover of darkness the trader's dog was killed by gunshot; the culprit was the Boy of the previous day's fiasco. Upon complaint by the trader, the soldier and an aid killed the first village dog they met. Then they called for all dogs, some thousand or so, to be brought for execution to expiate the crime. Ready hands appeared immediately and would have proceeded to the slaughter except for the trader's last-minute intervention to prevent an act which would have left the women of the village without transport for the many minor hauling duties about camp. Nearly half a century later Parkman, traveling with a camp of Oglalas far to the west along the front of the mountains, noted a similar incident. One man of the camp had received a present from another, who expected to get a mule in return. When the gift was reciprocated, the wife of the donor was outraged. It was her riding mule; furthermore, the original gift had been a dress for a rival wife, not for her. The two wives fell to fighting, and continued despite the floggings administered by the husband. Exasperated by this series of contretemps, the badgered husband, in a fury, went out and killed seven of his own horses. "What a bump of destructiveness," Parkman observed. "This is the sort of passion that often drives an Indian to his exploits of desperate courage." [19]

The contrast between these incidents and a comparable situation among the Pawnees reveals much concerning the

[19] Parkman, 1947, vol. 2, p. 437, June 12, 1846.

basic difference of horticultural social structure and its imple-
mentation. During Major Long's visit to the Plains, one of his
parties lost some of their supplies and horses through the
action of a group of Republican Pawnee Boys who got out of
the control of their leader. Later at a council meeting with the
Grand Pawnees the government agent pointedly cautioned the
chief against such behavior. Having already carefully established the fact that he was not personally intimidated by the
whites, the chief dealt with the Boys of his villages in just
the type of meeting in which challenging them would raise
the most resentment.

Instead of immediate reply, Tarrarecawaho, who alone had remained standing, addressed his warriors in a loud, fluent, and
impassionate manner: "I am the only individual of this nation that
possesses knowledge of the manners and powers of the whites. I have
been to the town of the Red Head (Governor Clark at St. Louis) and
saw there all that a red-skin could see. Here sits a chief (pointing to
the agent) who controls everything in this land; if he should pro-
hibit you from wearing breechcloths, you could not wear them. You
know that we cannot dispense with powder and balls; you must also
know that we cannot dispense with this chief, as he can prevent us
from obtaining them. I have no personal fear; I only dread the
consequences of improper conduct to the women and children; take
pity on your women and children, warriors. When he tells you that
he is a chief, he speaks truly; when he says that his soldiers appear
like grass in the spring, in place of those who die, he speaks truly;
you, my nation, are like a fly in strength, just so easily can his
mighty nation crush you between their fingers. You men, I have
done; tomorrow I will invite the American chief to council, and if
any of you wish to speak to him then, you have my consent. Do as I
do; I am not ashamed of what I have done; follow my example." [20]

[20] James, 1905, vol. 15, pp. 147–49.

The next day a meeting assembled with the chiefs and United States representatives on the dais above the mass of seated commoners. The performance was dominated by the high-ranking men. Gifts to the chief flowed along the usual channels down to commoners, with the chief retaining "only the United States flag," according to the principle that the best belonged to the highest. The Boys had to remain satisfied with a minor role. Toward the end of the meeting a subchief said that "if agreeable to his father (the Government Agent) he would return in a reasonable time, and bring some of his young warriors, for the purpose of performing a dance." The issue faded off into an amorphous cloud with which no one, let alone the Boys, could have successfully come to grips. The episode illustrates a strict channeling of authority, handled with such finesse that one gets the impression of well-oiled off-stage machinery determining that each actor perform his role in exact accordance with established precedent. The technique of diverting attention is classical.

There is concurrence in Parkman's Journal. His associate, Henry, told him that "the Pawnees are much more subordinate to their chiefs than the Sioux [Oglala] . . . that a chief [i.e., a partisan] of the former can with impunity whip one of the young men, but if a Sioux chief does it, he is sure to have some of his horses killed."[21]

Very different behavior among Dakotas of high status is suggested in Tabeau's sketch of a Bois Brule chief. Despite his position as the leader of one of the largest bands, this man presented a vacillating manner. On the same day he might be fainthearted and then audacious, fear-struck and bold, proud of his position and then servile, at the same time a troublemaker

[21] Parkman, 1947, vol. I, p. 434.

and a peace-seeker. Having fixed prices of advantage to the trader, the leader then might encourage his followers to demand reduced prices: "His is a character, hard, discontented with all and with himself, fidgety, ambitious in the extreme. Having neither the prudence nor the courage necessary to elevate himself, he is without perseverance in the methods he employs so unskillfully." The pages that follow are enriched with incidents of petty thefts, intrigues leading to the death of rivals, and various activities detrimental to the traders' parties. Throughout runs the snarled thread of the man's inner conflicts. In a final episode the chief, walking with a fellow leader, comes across a woman whose favor he has been seeking, to no avail. Impetuously he attempts to take his revenge by shooting her. The gun misses fire three or so times. Whereupon his companion remarks, "This is enough; you see that the gun does not wish to fire," or, as Tabeau himself laconically notes elsewhere, "A Savage who plans murder, keeps his gun well in order." [22]

This, then, is the type of individual who was pouring westward over the Plains astride the horse, whom Kroeber characterized as producing "a late high pressure center of culture," who would impress all observers with a culture which in its brief period of flowering was indeed ornate. It may be that in an eagerness to demonstrate the values of the native ways of life on the Great Plains, anthropologists have glorified the mode of existence of the nomadic peoples. In this they may have been abetted by the people themselves in recollections of a kind of "Golden Age," a colorful and exciting time of youth and freedom, which of course may never have existed in quite such beautiful contours. In sober fact the life of the nomads had

[22] Tabeau, 1939, pp. 111, 112, 115.

little of stability about it. They were frequently in desperate straits from which they rescued themselves only by dependence on the surplus food of the villages. Having once committed themselves to the horse and bison, they were increasingly drawn into a new and dynamically imbalanced situation. Many factors were at work. The most basic, if not apparent at an early date, was the appearance of Europeans as harbingers of a new economy which would ultimately disrupt and reorient all native modes of life.

Paramount among the new European items was the domesticated horse. However, there was not immediate access to this self-perpetuating, self-repairing, and essentially self-maintaining adjunct to native hunting practices. Horses were first seen in the mid-sixteenth century in the trains of De Soto and, more particularly, Coronado. Yet a century passed before we find reference to these animals in native hands. Opinion now relegates the adoption of the horse to the eighteenth century.[23] As noted above, the French report horses in considerable numbers among the Caddos at the end of the seventeenth century. The Pawnees and Wichitas brought horses from the Spanish settlements in short order. And Bourgmont, two decades later, bargained with the Kansas for mounts en route to the Padoucas to the west, who already had considerable herds.

Horses also moved northward along the western flanks of the mountains into the Pacific Northwest. A trade was soon developed across the passes into the Plains. By 1734 the Mandans were reported to have horses. The La Vérendrye parties,

[23] Wissler, 1914; Webb, 1931; Haines, 1938a, 1938b; Swanton, 1939. Ewers, 1955, pp. 1–15, reviews the data and adds new material.

some six years later, were told of horses among the "Pananas and the Pananis" some distance downstream. They were said to have come from the Spaniards. Now mounts were coming from the Columbian Plateau country; the La Vérendryes report numbers of horses among the Gens de Chevaux and the Gens du Serpent on the western Plains.

After the 1750s the animals were common enough along the Missouri River to allow of regular trade to the east and northeast. At the turn of the century horses were so commonplace among the Arikaras and Mandans as to cause no special comment by either Tabeau or Lewis and Clark. Nevertheless, the latter felt moved to list some ten westerly tribes which "bring horses and robes" to the trade, and more specifically to mention that the Cheyennes "steal horses from the Spanish Settlements."[24] The changes brought about in the total life of the people were enormous and cannot be here reviewed. Nevertheless, consideration of some of the details is in order.

If we consider only the bison herds we can see something of the nature of the changes. Access to the horse vastly increased the hunting range and the amount of meat that could be transported. Greater numbers of animals were slaughtered each year and more hunters were involved. Aside from migrations and normal drifting, there was an overall movement of the animals to the west. Tabeau heard from the Arikaras, on a midwinter passage from the Mandan villages, that over some ninety leagues along the Missouri they had traveled through a single scattered herd. Cheyennes coming some seventy leagues from the Black Hills reported the same condition in that direction,

[24] Tabeau, 1939, passim, for interesting details; Lewis and Clark, 1904–1905, vol. 1, pp. 176, 190.

and the Dakotas said that the prairies to the east of the river were covered for some forty leagues. [25]

There were still many bison along the east bank of the river in 1830. Denig says the Yanktonai Dakotas were able to kill fifteen hundred buffalo in a single surround opposite Fort Pierre. The count was determined from the number of tongues traded to the company agents as the hunters returned from the kill. Yet by the late 1840s the country east of the river was nearly empty of bison. They had gradually moved west and north-west, and now were to be found mainly along the Grand and the headwaters of the other streams flowing into the Missouri. The herds never abandoned the country of the Crow Indians until their final extermination. These bison in southeastern Montana and the Big Horn country of eastern Wyoming were basic to the security enjoyed by the Crows for many years, but they were also a primary reason for continual warfare and raiding by the Blackfeet and western Dakotas. [26]

In addition, there was the demand for bison robes and hides. This increased hunting must also have increased the difficulty of the hunt. The herds would become more wary and less settled in their habits, adding to their tendency to drift. There were also increased pressures from the west as the Nez Percés, Flatheads, Shoshones, Comanches, and other tribes moved out onto the Plains. The whole matter ended with the systematic extermination of the animals at the hands of United States hunters during the extensive military operations in the decades after the Civil War. [27]

[25] Tabeau, 1939, pp. 70–71 and n 3.
[26] Denig, 1961, pp. 25, 30, 193–204 passim.
[27] Roe, 1951, pp. 447–66, reviews and comments on these events.

Even at the opening of the nineteenth century, while the bison were abundant, life was far from secure. Tabeau tells of a famine among the Brule and other Dakota groups in November and December, 1804:

It was partly due to the Indians having deprived themselves in our favor of more than a thousand pieces of dried meat, but this quantity would have supplied food for only a few days longer for eight or nine hundred mouths. . . . The Sioux, the Cheyennes, and other wandering nations reckon everything from the periods in which famine has made terrible ravages among them.[28]

Given a food supply so precarious, the nomads were forced to look for permanent sources of supply during the lean months— that furnished by the labor of the horticultural groups. With his usual perception Tabeau noted succinctly that the Dakotas had "in the Ricarnas, a certain kind of serf, who cultivates for them and who, as they say, take, for them, the place of women."[29]

Another European import, the gun, has been considered to be equivalent or simply analogous to the horse in its role among the native peoples of the Plains. Such a view does not give us a real understanding of the matter. The gun, in striking contrast to the horse, is not a complete and self-sufficient tool. It results from a complex manufacturing process and, through its necessary accessories, remains intimately tied to the industrial society which produced it. The horse was readily available from native sources, but the gun immediately brought a close relationship with a permanent source of supply, ultimately European. The line led directly back to the factories

[28] Tabeau, 1939, pp. 71–72.
[29] Ibid., p. 130.

responsible not only for the gun and its constituent parts but, more important, the indispensible chemical explosives. The native user was with difficulty able to repair, perhaps even to maintain, his new tool, but without accessory supplies the gun was not even a good club. Powder was perishable and was always maintained in small amounts by the supplier. The man with the gun was at the mercy of the European, at however great remove.

Nor was this weapon a perfected tool until a late date. The muskets, fowling pieces, and the Northwest guns of the seventeenth and eighteenth centuries combined short range and poor accuracy with single-load action and flintlock firing mechanisms. Fully dependable rifles were not available until far into the nineteenth century. Even then, as always, castoff models, inferior designs, and poor quality merchandise were the stock in trade of the Indian market. Thus we find traders at the opening of the nineteenth century advising their superiors that the Missouri trade would not support great numbers of guns: "For this [bison] hunt they rightly prefer the bow and arrow to our guns and ammunition. If they desire the latter, it is for war alone, as they do not even dare to use them against the black bear." The effect of a misfire in the face of a bear's charge is readily appreciated. So also is the difficulty with which guns could be loaded and fired in the excited and confused milling of a buffalo herd.

It is unlikely that the gun swept like a wave across the Plains, nor did the native peoples everywhere accept it immediately as an unmitigated boon. The bow lasted alongside the gun for many decades. The two weapons together may well have served different functions. As late as 1798 the Mandans were using flint-tipped weapons. Their favorite was the spear, tipped with iron on the rare occasions when they could get it. David Thompson tells us that their guns were few in proportion to the number of men, "for they have no supplies" save those brought by infrequent visiting traders. His crew traded seven of their ten guns to the villagers. He notes in passing that the bullhide shields of these people were proof against arrows and spears but were useless against balls. Less than a decade later, Henry, with the same people, noted specifically that arms and ammunition "are . . . necessary articles [for defense], and everyone has a stock of balls and powder laid up in case of emergency." [30]

None of the defects seriously mar its use in certain kinds of armed conflict. These instruments would be very attractive as weapons of defense against raiding and looting, especially were a resident trader available. Among the nomadic peoples, unless close sources of supply were maintained, the problem of carting along such awkward paraphernalia may have outweighed the gun's advantage as a weapon of offense. One would expect that on the Missouri it was for long less an adjunct to the raider and more an asset to the village defenders.

Native conflict here seldom approximated European ideas of war. Village autonomy and the absence of large political units make wars for territorial gains unlikely. The Cheyenne, Dakota, or even Blackfoot party raiding into Crow country was not met by frontier guards and standing armies. Clashes were rather those of small patrols, raids, or hunting parties surprised and dealt with as an immediate expediency. A constant motive for conflict was the looting of the villagers' food stores; this was

[30] Ibid., p. 163; Thompson, 1962, p. 173; Henry and Thompson, 1897, vol. 1, p. 330. For further and often differing opinion, see Secoy, 1953; Hanson, 1955; Hamilton, 1960; Russell, 1962, 1967.

real economic war, but there was no intent to seize and use the enemies' means of production. If the goods could not be got by gift or barter, the raid was always there; or a raid might be tried just for the chance of it—if successful, so much the better; if not, the same raiders could appear a few days later as traders or beggars. Strategic positions were not seized and held, nor territories invaded and occupied. There was no intent to further the glory of any great political unit. If glory was sought, it was the glory of the individual: a Boy on his way up, stealing horses or striking a defiant pose in the face of an attacker, touching a dead enemy at the imminent risk of his own death; or a mourning survivor seeking personal vengeance for the death or mutilation of a relative. All of this is but one side of the coin. The other is the problem of defense and retaliation which muddies the clear water of motive in so many situations involving aggressive action. Defense and retaliation must have been endless in all those groups. The more the horses and the fewer the bison, the more penetration of new regions and raiding of new stores; the more deaths and disasters, the more would defense and retaliation increase.

The food resources of the horticulturalists also reflected the changing conditions. There was the direct demand of the trade for the products themselves. In addition the labor of the women was diverted into channels of hide working and the production of other commodities for the trade. The failure of food crops, any unusual demands on the stored surpluses, such as raids by nomads, would empty the storage cists of their irreplaceable surplus. The horticulturalists themselves now operated close to the subsistence minimum for their own needs. Tabeau on May 24, 1804, found things to be in a dangerous condition at the lower Arikara village. When the corn crops failed, which was not unusual, the bison could be an uncertain source of food for the villagers. The herds must be continuously followed to lay in surplus supplies, but this was impossible because of the demands of horticulture. The villagers left for the hunt only when supplies ran low. He found that there were remaining in the town only a few old people, who were subsisting on "pear flowers," sweet grass, the bark of young willows, and other herbage. The hunters had failed for two months to find sufficient meat. The desperate situation would continue until the first squash became edible. Straggling families came into the village after having spent three months on the prairies in a condition of fasting due to the absence of game. Tabeau and others noted with some alarm a practice of all the village tribes. During the spring thaw numerous bison, drowned during the previous fall and winter, were released from the ice and came floating past the villages. The villagers, excellent swimmers, would retrieve the carcasses. The hides were of little use and, as Denig noted, the flesh was in such high condition as to be dipped with a spoon. Yet it served as a welcome source of food and the Indians were inordinately fond of it during its season. Such meat could not be preserved, and was actually in very short supply.[31]

The Arikaras were suffering a population decline at this time. The effects of epidemics and continual warfare on the internal social structure of the village must have been felt throughout the total socio-economic fabric and must have been especially severe in the area of food production. Thus the nomads operated in an ecological situation that was out of balance. The margin of exploitation which the horse offered them was slim at best if they were constantly faced with the

[31] Tabeau, 1939, p. 74; Denig, 1961, p. 49. Mackenzie in Masson, 1889–90, vol. 1, p. 366, adds further detail.

threat of periods of starvation. Their expanding society involved population increases, and the bison herds, which had earlier seemed endless, were not sufficient for the needs of the growing groups. Such food surpluses as the horticulturalists had were available to the nomads through various other channels.

In addition to raiding, native trade offered access to these products. Such trade always remained on a basis of barter, partaking of the quality of gift exchange and honoring, but this does not detract from its very real economic function. This was an exchange of commodities for the mutual benefit of both parties, regardless of sharp practices that might be followed. The village Indians were noted as traders of established reputation by the earliest observers. The trade was not so much between the villages inter alia, but far more consistently between the villages and the visiting nomadic or European groups. Jean Baptiste Trudeau, visiting the Arikara country in the 1790s, noted:

They maintain a partial trade with their oppressors, the Teton, to whom they barter horses, mules, corn, beans and a species of tobacco which they cultivate; and receive in return guns, ammunition, kettles, axes, and other articles which the Tetons obtain from the Yanktons of N. and Sissatones, who trade with Mr. Cammeron, on the river St. Peters. These horses and mules the Ricaras obtain from their western neighbors, who visit them frequently for the purpose of trafficking.[32]

This was a trade involving staple goods with stated market times. In the fourth decade of the previous century the La Vérendryes found among the Mandans a flourishing trade in bison robes and corn involving western nomadic groups,

[32] Trudeau, 1914, pp. 472–74.

probably Blackfoot. Several tribes, to the number of two hundred lodges or more, came on horseback, bringing skins dressed in colored porcupine quills and plumage, as well as white buffalo robes, in exchange for corn and beans, of which the villagers were in ample supply. Trade with the Assiniboins was by then an established matter. They left during the summers to take European trade items south to the villages in exchange for corn and beans. In addition the Mandans offered tobacco, dressed skins, and colored feathers. The nature of the relationship is indicated by La Vérendrye: "The Mandan are much more crafty than the Assiniboine in their commerce and in everything, and always dupe them."

Tabeau furnishes great detail concerning the trade between the Arikaras and the nomadic groups at the dawn of the nineteenth century. He notes that the Arikaras have to endure the presence of the Dakotas for much of the year. The groups settled around the villages during the winter absorbed any advantages that came to the Arikaras from the summer trade. However, in trade with the Cheyennes, the Arikaras benefited themselves in furnishing corn, tobacco, beans, squash, and other garden produce, for which they received products of the hunt in nearly equal amounts. During the decade before, the Arikaras had been in the custom of traveling to a fair at the foot of the Black Hills where they met visitors from eight other wandering tribes in addition to their friends, the Cheyennes. That these fairs attracted considerable numbers is indicated by Tabeau's account of some fifteen hundred to sixteen hundred men among the visitors to the Arikaras at the beginning of August, 1804.[33]

[33] La Vérendrye, 1927, pp. 253–54, 323–24; Tabeau, 1939, pp. 154, 162–63.

Shortly after this date Henry mentions the extensive trade which the Cheyennes, encamped one day's journey up the Little Missouri, conducted with the Mandan villages. Bringing turkey tail feathers in great numbers, they bartered for ammunition and other European goods, as well as the staple food items. Large parties came, bringing dried meat, robes, furs, and leather goods dressed in a fashion particularly attractive to the villagers and ornamented with fancy porcupine quill work. Horses to trade were also brought along. Cache pits were opened which might contain twenty to thirty bushels of corn and beans. A twelve-month supply of food had been thus laid up by the villagers in addition to surpluses for the trade. All of this bustle and preparatory activity took place in the face of a threatened attack by three hundred Tetons and Yanktons hoping to plunder the very supplies being traded to the Cheyennes. The Dakota raiding party was turned away, but not without leaving some thirty dead.[34]

Another trader, Larocque, visited the Hidatsa villages en route to verify rumors of untapped beaver resources among the Crows. He was importuned to abandon his plans and trade his goods for Hidatsa horses; the trail would be dangerous and the Crows filled with treachery. Learning of the impending arrival of some two thousand Crows, the trader concluded that his hosts merely desired "to have the whole trade themselves." He wished also to avoid setting precedents or granting controls which the Hidatsas might exploit were new sources of fur to develop. Now he was befriended by the local chief, Le Borgne, who assured his protection and free passage. This man had a Crow "son," the chief, Red Calf, duly adopted in the ceremony

[34] Henry and Thompson, 1897, vol. 1, pp. 355–56, 359–63. Jablow, 1951, amplifies trade relations.

of the pipe, or calumet, who would in turn befriend the traveler:

When the Mountain Indians arrive, be kind to them, they know not white men; you will hand them your pipe of ceremony; you will clothe the chief; you will give him a flag and a stem, and you will make him a present, for he is a great man.

Thus Red Calf would become in turn the son of Larocque, whose safety would be assured. Such an arrangement would advantage the fur company, since the purely native trade was considerable. Larocque was impressed with the "incredible" quantity of European goods which the Missouri River tribes amassed through native channels.

On the day set for trading, the hosts offered the newly arrived Crows the pipe and, as presents, 200 guns with 100 rounds of ammunition each, 100 bushels of corn, plus quantities of kettles, axes, cloth, and other European items. The visitors in their turn offered 250 horses, large packets of bison robes, buckskin shirts, leggings, dried meat, and other produce of their own manufacture. The innocence of the Crows to European goods was further demonstrated by their use of stone tools. In addition they dressed their beaver pelts in a fashion to ruin them for the trade, but quite in accord with ancient native practice.

The rate of exchange was validated by formalized dancing, in which the neighboring Mandans were included. However, the final arrangements for Larocque's departure reveals flaws in Le Borgne's plans. The Crows were far from unanimous in a desire for trade emissaries. A voluble faction had considerable realistic fears that contact with the Europeans would throw evil medicine among them. The friendly faction felt constrained to warn of the real danger of attack at the hands of the dissidents en route to the Crow fastnesses.[35]

Such commerce continued past the middle of the century with increasing amounts allotted to the fur trade. But the native trade with the nomads went on unabated. In the late 1850s Denig noted that the Arikaras raised great quantities of corn at the village near old Fort Clark. The Sioux, fond of corn and needing provisions, maintained peace with the Arikaras, to whom they traded meat and skins. The advantage was general; any family with the necessary commodity could barter for corn, dried squash, and other foods. Thus there was no real cause for quarrels, and minor differences were lost in the interests of the better-disposed majority. There is no doubt that this pattern had an ancient basis; at least a century of native trade along these lines can be documented.[36]

Once in the hands of the equestrian nomads, food and trade goods alike did not go to maintain a stratified social structure with its attendant elaborations. The Dakota ideal was individualistic in the extreme, and each biological family formed an independent unit that might shift its allegiances when desired. The shibboleth of giving as found here had different consequences than among the horticultural peoples. After a lucky raid a family might suddenly find itself rich with an abundance of horses. True, this wealth would shortly be given to others,

[35] Laroque, 1910, p. 20. Masson, 1888–89, vol. 1, p. 344, offer two versions of the same event with a detailed rendering of speeches. Lowie, 1914, incidentally notes the Arikara origin of the dance and its relation to the Pawnee *hako;* Bowers, 1965, offers a generalized account of the dance from informants, but does not note our sources.

[36] Denig, 1961, pp. 35–36.

but there were no stable ranked groups to channel its flow. The fortunate family might raise its status to the highest in the group by the mere fact of making itself poor in giving. Shortly there would be gifts from others who in turn were raising their own status. The distribution of wealth among the Dakotas raised the level of the whole group. There was no village unit to be maintained with the labor of the members. There was no hereditary group to whom the wealth was funneled before it found its way unevenly back down to the others. There was no bar to the complete social mobility of any member within the group. Even the "simplest soldier" could climb to the top of the ladder, and even he could defy the chief. Although a position of hereditary chief is reported by some observers, this post of itself carried less prestige and actual authority than it was possible to achieve through individual effort. The ranking of leaders shifted with the fortunes of given men, resulting in a plethora of leaders vying with each other for the allegiance of followers, of many small groups with little stability of allegiance and considerable mobility of residence.

The contrast with horticultural patterns is exemplified by Bradbury's observations along the Missouri in 1811. Having passed the Omahas and Poncas with some difficulty, the party faced a group of Dakotas who had waited eleven days to intercept the shipments bound for the Arikaras. The group consisted of one Yankton tribe and two of the Tetons, yet it totaled only 280 lodges. When a parley was called to consult with the two hundred warriors, fourteen chiefs were sent to represent them. This abundance of chiefs is in striking contrast to the number present at a Pawnee village when Long's party arrived. They were greeted by between three and four hundred mounted Indians [warriors] . . . rushing around us in every direction . . . with loud shouts and yells. The few whom we had observed in advance of the main body, and whom as they came near we recognized to be the chief men presented a perfect contrast to the others in their slow movements and simplicity of dress. . . .

and then, during the parade to the village,

Latelesha, the grand chief, perceiving that the division of his warriors that were on our left, raised some dust, ordered them all to the leeward, that we might not be incommoded.[37]

The very instability of allegiance, leadership, and habitation of the nomads gave them important advantages both in warfare and in the changes that were occurring. By contrast, all efforts to preserve the horticultural village as a stable physical unit were actually contributing to its vulnerability to attack. Furthermore, the wealth of these villages had to be distributed in a way that would preserve their inner social structure. If the village were to continue, the total corn complex had to be maintained. Its maintenance assured also the total retention of the superstructure of the priest and the chief. The Dakota chief, a violent figure of war and aggression, was a leader who met the demands of the period. The authority figure of the horticulturalists was obliged to remain calm and remote from the very struggle which was threatening his existence and that of the people. Within the village the Boys stood against the Dakotas under the leadership of some striving brave. These men were subordinate contributors, not village leaders.

[37] Bradbury, 1904, pp. 103 ff.; James, 1905, vol. 15, p. 150.

125

Yet not all contacts between the nomads and the horticulturalists were violent; alliances were formed, brittle though they might be. In the fall of 1807 the Arikaras halted Ensign Pryor's official government party on its way upstream to the Mandans, with whom the Arikaras and some Dakota allies were fighting. The council that was held and the battle which followed saw the Dakotas in active partnership with the Arikaras, although this alliance would probably be broken the next spring.[38] Through all this shifting picture of wars and allegiances the theme of weakening horticultural resistance remains constant. Even so there was a complex cultural interchange between horticulturalists and nomads. It can best be understood if the total nomad society is visualized as a counterpart to that segment of the horticultural social ordering which contained the achieved statuses and was the arena of social advancement for commoners. Dancing fraternities, military rankings, and vision-validated religious ceremonies or groupings were common to the two cultures. It is as though the socio-political structure of the nomads had not developed above the level of the highest-ranking commoners or Boys among the horticulturalists. Or to put it another way, if the horticultural complex and all of its structural ramifications were abstracted from the villages, there would remain both the subsistence pattern and the socio-political organization of the nomads. It was this social structure and aspect of culture which effloresced in the hands of the nomads to produce the characteristics of "typical Plains culture." The parvenus and the climbers within the horticultural villages must also have contributed to this efflorescence. Certainly all of the elaborations found in the religious system of the nomads were present in the horticul-

[38] Chittenden, 1929, vol. I, pp. 120–24.

tural villages among those men, and they were the likely vehicle for interchange between the two patterns.

In keeping with the individualistic emphases of the people, Dakota religion was a matter of personal inventiveness in which the propitiation of the powers resulted in visions which would give the individual unique powers. There were few basic elaborations which would bring this individualistic system into the stable and organized form of the horticultural villages. The very physical nature of village life assured that no member was ever far from the control of the religious system which gave the total culture meaning. Among the nomads religion was more of a private matter. There were of course great communal ceremonies like the sun dance which so impressed the early observers with its masochistic excesses. But even in this ceremony we most frequently find the desires of the individual stressed as a center around which the great social event was focused.

The principal patterns of the personal vision quest which was so important in nomad religion have been summarized and analyzed by Benedict for the whole of aboriginal North America. She observed that although the animal patrons of the doctors in the horticultural villages were the foundation for the total doctors' organization, the seeking of personal visions frequently failed. Furthermore, the power one received from the animal lodge was achieved not so much by a trance state in which visions came as through the memorization of specific instructions from the practicing doctor, who was the initiate's father-tutelary. She contrasts the Dakota situation where doctors had to secure their independent, personal visions through their own efforts by fasting and other forms of propitiation, even though they afterward joined organizations on the basis of their supernatural experiences. The complete absence of any priest figure among the Dakotas was associated with the absence of a truly codified theology.[39]

Personal visions were also present among the horticulturalists. The Arikaras give descriptions of adolescent vision quests, although self-torture was not a part of them. With the exception of the Mandan-Hidatsas, self-torture among the horticulturalists appears muted and associated primarily with mourning. Personal visions were utilized to validate many of the Pawnee organizations; however, those very societies which were validated by visions alone were the ones classified by Murie as "private organizations." From his account it is evident that they were rather ephemeral societies organized by commoners in order to gain prestige within the village. They were indeed a part of Pawnee religion, but in this context, they deviate from the organized, supported, and recognized religious forms. Individual members of these societies, and even whole societies of this type, were sometimes in actual overt conflict with the status quo.[40] The vision-validated organization had both a different social function and different value than it possessed among the Dakotas. The contrast is understandable. If the established horticultural leaders were to encourage the uncontrolled invention of "new" religious forms by the parvenus on the foundation of their new wealth of horses and many war exploits, the village as an integrated unit would not last long. Among the Dakotas such achievements would simply add to the success of the total group and not run counter to its "best interests."

[39] Benedict, 1922; see also Fortune, 1932.

[40] Benedict, 1922, pp. 6, 9; Bradbury, 1904, p. 115; Murie, 1914, p. 579 and passim; Maximilian, 1906, vol. 23, p. 390; Lowie, 1915; Weltfish, 1965, pp. 318–31.

Although the personal vision and its organizational aspects were present among the horticulturalists, and had long been so, it represented a muted aspect of life which depended upon the restless commoners for its elaboration and use. In a sense the horticultural religion held encysted within itself an old individualistic structure which was in close affinity with the total religion of the nomads. With regard to specific shared religious elements, we may never know who invented and who imitated, especially since many of the elements must have been anciently shared. Nevertheless, the affinity must have formed a fertile ground for the interchange of ideas and elements in periods when these peoples were in close contact. It is as though the new crosscutting of interests related the parvenus more closely to the nomads than to the leader families of their own villages.

Among the Arikaras, Boys who joined with the nomads against the interests of the village were driven from the group. In 1806 an Arikara chief explained to Lewis and Clark why peace had not been kept, saying that "they had some bad young men [Boys] who would not listen to the councels [of Lewis and Clark] but would join with the Seioux, those men they had discarded and drove out of their villages."[41] The horticultural upper ranks were forced to take steps which weakened the strength of their village. Such alignments with the nomads must have contributed frequently to the continued dwindling of the villages.

In this setting the function, origin, and spread of the sun dance may be considered. Veneration of the tree in the Pawnee Four-Pole Ceremony and Grandmother Cedar among the Arikaras; the plan and orientation of the earth-lodge temple,

[41] Lewis and Clark, 1904–1905, vol. 5, p. 352, Aug. 21, 1806.

echoed in the sun dance arbor and altar; the nest, or bundle, of the Pawnee Hako, reflected in the sun dance bundle; the self-torture of the Mandan Okipa; perhaps even the veneration of the sun—all well-integrated religious elements among the villagers—indicate that they furnished much of the building material for this late cult, spread far and wide by the equestrian nomads.[42] Where this ceremony occurred among the horticulturalists it would have appealed to the parvenus; elements of it may have actually been "invented" by them, utilizing forms already existing in the official religion. Once invented or borrowed, it would have been accorded the recognition which the religious hierarchy would give to any popular new cult.

The conditions facing the horticulturalists after the turn of the nineteenth century may now be summarized. The villages in their position of favored middlemen for the expanding European forces were beset with myriad problems. Pressure from displaced native groups against the easternmost of these horticulturalists, the sedentary Siouan peoples, was reflected in increasing conflict with the Caddoan villages.

The villages were dwindling in population and were fractured by internal social strains; they were threatened from without and within. On the other hand, the nomads found with the horse a new way of life and new powers. Among the Teton Dakotas at least, trade ties no longer meant labor spent in hunting on foot for the dwindling fur supplies for the European market. Native trade along the Missouri was in new terms. Although food supplies were precarious on the Plains, the horse added a form of insurance, increasing the hunting range

[42] Spier, 1921; Fletcher, 1904; Lesser, 1933; Weltfish, 1965; Curtis, 1909; Catlin, 1967. Bennett, 1944, also speculates on this subject.

and making available more time for horse raiding. More horses meant more food supplies from the villages. In many respects this was a totally new mode of existence for the Dakotas and one which allowed of continuing expansion for the people as a whole.

The horticultural villages were faced with depopulation, increasing warfare, decreasing food stores, social unrest, and many factors which threatened their internal stability in the face of the more monolithic if less stable social organization of the nomads. The Caddoan-speaking peoples, in their dwindling villages, were held by the weight of ancient traditions which had once offered the most successful solution to the problem of life in the Plains environment. The combining of village remnants weakened the leader families and contributed to defeat by the nomads. Consider the unenviable position of a chief with the remnants of his own people joining an established village. The flow of gratuities, the religious and economic prerogatives, in effect, his very existence, depended upon his status within his own village. That status rested upon the fealty of followers, ensured by the uninterrupted flow of gifts. But the chief of the host village would demand his own and his peoples' share in this flow. The new relationship would automatically call for a reorientation of allegiance, a revision in the channeling of the flow of wealth. Such a conflict between Arikara leaders was witnessed by Tabeau during his visit.

The chief, Man Crow (Kakawita), was in an uncomfortable situation as head of an autonomous village forced now to join the village of Sawahaini under its head chief, Sitting Crow (Kakawissassa). Man Crow's following was small, and he must have found himself in competition with Sitting Crow, yet he conducted himself with self-assurance and was always the chief in manner during the months of Tabeau's residence. His machinations were carefully set within the framework of chiefly behavior and protocol. He maneuvered to have Tabeau live in his house rather than with the head chief, Sitting Crow. The economic advantages would help to outweigh the weakness of the remnants of his village. Man Crow was able to convince Tabeau that it was he who should be sent to the Mandan village to meet Lewis and Clark and receive the coveted official United States medal, although

the discord and envy of the chiefs, even of those most zealous for peace, prevent the departure, so necessary, of Kakawita [Man Crow]. They fear lest he receive too many honors among the Mandanes and particularly some marks of distinction on the part of Captn Lewis, who has his winter quarters there.

Man Crow made the trip, received the honors, and no doubt raised himself considerably.

In all of the arguments and plots and counterplots which came as a result of Tabeau's residence in the village, Man Crow carefully advanced his own cause. He supported the deviant behavior of Tabeau through charges of tightfistedness and other "unchiefly" behavior, even to the extent of distributing gifts of his own to the disgruntled villagers. However, in the final debacle which resulted in Tabeau's departure, Man Crow was forced to preserve the solid front of the upper ranks. Tabeau's characterization of him reveals much:

This Savage, of whom I have often had an occasion to speak, is proud, alert, ferocious, cruel, and, consequently a great man. . . . He is firm and constant, when he has taken sides, more intelligent than he appeared at first, frank and without subterfuge, he declares at once his dissent. Although exacting as a Ricara, he waits until one offers to him and does not debase himself by continual begging. . . . [He] declared only once against me—in the general uprising of which I am going to speak. Besides he had warned me.

When faced with the alternative of coming into open conflict with the leaders in the host village or suffering personal disadvantage, Man Crow chose the latter. He declared against Tabeau. In so doing he prevented an open break in the ranks of the leader families, although he must have lost considerable economic advantage for himself.[43]

Similar conflicts must have been common in the other villages of this period. When Trudeau arrived on the upper Missouri in 1795 he found only a part of the Arikaras there. The others had broken away because of rivalry between chiefs. The fact that they were later to return indicates the way affiliations shifted. Other disagreements within the horticultural groups were being intensified. Among the Caddoan-speaking peoples the Boys and the commoners were offered new opportunities. Warfare was becoming more frequent, important, and intense. The war ladder, while crowded, offered increasing opportunities for status climbing, and the climbers were gaining in confidence. There is abundant evidence that chiefs sometimes found it difficult to restrain rebellious activities even within the village itself. Murie mentions one such case. When the ancient mores were broken by the society of Young Dogs, who seized sacred meat while policing the village, they were immediately removed from office and the regular Lance Soldiers resumed authority. These Boys offered as their defense the fact that they had been to the west where they had seen people among whom

[43] Tabeau, 1939, pp. 129–37, passim.

all shared and shared alike. But even with its internal dissension the village held together. When the horticulturalists went to war they carried the figurative weight of the stable village around their necks as they, in all reality, often wore as a talisman a sacred ear of corn, to bring them success on a raid.[44]

It is true that the status striving of the commoners tended to be conducted in the individualistic setting which was the ideal among the equestrian warriors. Yet any wealth which they brought back would be absorbed into the intravillage flow of goods along established lines. If such striving was successful, rewards were given to the individual in a fashion to align him with the leaders. Thus the more successful were the individual strivings of the lower ranks, the more their potential leaders were isolated and removed from their ambit of interests. In effect, these men were constantly being siphoned off to a higher level where they were negated as a threat or even made allies by those concerned with the maintenance of the status quo. All this was reinforced by the dogmas of the religion. In his very achievements on the warpath the warrior figure of the horticultural villages honored Mother Corn and the village bundle.

The village organization was also supported by the women as a large conservative faction. In her capacity as a producer of foodstuffs even the humblest woman was aligned with the upper ranks and the religion which supported it. When the village was abandoned temporarily, the women were in a constant fret to return and begin their gardening again. But the success of this planting and harvesting demanded the whole round of ceremonial activity, which in turn called for the

[44] Murie, 1914, pp. 595–99 ff.. Weltfish, 1965, pp. 332–46, has other examples.

maintenance of the total socio-economic structure that placed control in the hands of the leader families.

The priests were in an excellent position to carry out the wishes of the conservative elements of the village. Even the other means of food production, the communal hunt, was put in the terms of the old religion. On the bison hunt the Boys were held back from attacking the herd until the powers of the bundle said, through earthly intermediaries, that the time for striking had come. Murray, who hunted with the Pawnees in the 1830s, complained that

a good day for buffalo hunting was lost . . . owing to the superstitious folly of the Indians or rather, perhaps, to the intrigues of the chiefs. After going through a ceremony somewhat similar to the Heathen augury, the Great Spirit was declared by the medicine-men to be unpropitious for a hunt and most of the day was consumed in electing "soldiers" (3rd class or caste among the Pawnee). . . . On the 30th the Great Spirit was still unpropitious. . . . As far as I can learn, their idea of a Divinity is a single presiding Being or Spirit, *generally* benevolent, but changeable, according to the supplies or offerings which he receives of buffalo, of which they dedicate considerable portions to him. (No small part of this dedicated meat is consumed by the medicine-men.)

When the actual moment for the attack had come, the impatient and vocally rebellious young men were still restrained until an old man limped far ahead to carry out the mummery of "pointing the herd." The results of the hunt, as Murray suggests, would follow the old, established lines of distribution in the same fashion as the very inception and organization of the hunt had been phrased in religious concepts.[45]

[45] Murray, 1839, vol. I, pp. 233–36.

Some ten years earlier, during his tour of the prairies, Herzog Paul Wilhelm had pursued this general topic with a priest of the Skiri band of Pawnees:

I finally asked him whether he really believed that the ceremonies which the priests and old men made use of to protect their fields against the attacks of and destruction by hostile parties and wanton Boys, whether they were really of any value. The priest replied: "Great Father, if the enemies and the Boys did not believe in them, the old men would starve to death and the priests would perish." [46]

In all aspects of life affecting the basic livelihood of the people the leading families and the conservative elements within the village retained control of the results of the labor of the people. It is no mere symbol that the chief parceled out the land to the women leaders of the various families according to their need. The same pattern determined the way in which the Pawnee chiefs permanently allotted the lands in severalty. Significantly, Lesser has indicated that this was the final gesture, ultimately reducing the chiefs to a condition of economic equality with their followers, which broke their power. [47]

Throughout the history of the northern Caddoan horticulturalists the patterning of the total life of the village was such as never to allow a basic reorientation of socio-economic relations. Without this reorientation a transition to equestrian nomadism was impossible. The villages with their terribly reduced populations remained to the end as they were shown in the opening of this study: anomalous island remnants of the old, in an engulfing sea of the new equestrian nomadism,

[46] Paul Wilhelm, 1941, p. 440.
[47] Lesser, 1933, p. 46.

preserving the values which had been defined long ago for the conduct of human life on the Great Plains.

These people still live on, their culture broken, yet unassimilated within the industrialized culture of the United States. And still the secret of the old way of life was held tenaciously by some of them. In the late 1930s an old Arikara leader consistently refused to teach me religious secrets without the proper exorbitant fees. One day on the reservation when we were driving past a Christian mission residence we saw on the porch a benign, portly, contented figure, the very cigar in his mouth a symbol of affluence. Said my friend,

You see. That is the way it goes. Who has the fattest cows, who has the most expensive radio, who has the best car, the finest land, the warmest house and the best food on all of the reservation? It is he. And it is rightfully his. And this is how he comes by it: he has religious secrets which he alone knows. For access to these secrets the people must pay him much. That is the nature of the secrets. For this they keep him in luxury. He knows well that he cannot lavishly give away the very thing which gives him life. Thus I cannot let you know my secrets.

Conclusions

This study began with a consideration of the anomalous position held by the native horticultural peoples of the Plains in the classificatory systems of anthropologists. The horticultural pattern proved to be an ancient way of life. The problem of horticultural stability in the face of the equestrian nomadism was posed. The solution to that problem was not simple. At least three basic and constituent culture patterns were dynamically involved in the processes of culture change which culminated in the situation described by the ethnologists. Two of these, horticulture and nomadic hunting and gathering, were indigenous to the New World. The third pattern was that of a foreign culture, the civilization of Europe,

139

itself rapidly developing during the period in question. The data and approach in this book have been determined by this latter culture and may contain distortions.

The Europeans appeared in the New World with a pattern of colonialism which called for the exploitation of the movable wealth by the labor of the inhabitants, the final removal of the people, and the ultimate occupation and utilization of their land. In the beginning the Europeans were dependent upon the native peoples and exchanged culture elements which were to modify the native patterns considerably. The Europeans brought lines and bases of supply which they expanded until there was in the New World an offshoot of the Old World pattern which developed along its own lines, drawing strength from the native peoples and their land and resources. In the process of this change there were many concomitant changes in the native cultures of the Plains.

The pattern of native horticulture was a strong indigenous growth developing out of deep prehistoric roots. The most characteristic integrated features of this society were nascent class stratification and an elaborate religious system. Stable leadership was predominantly hereditary; at the apex of the social structure was the chief, the civic leader of a stable community whose position and prerogatives were sanctioned by the religion. The social structure was justified and the permanent village held together by the cyclical religious regulation of all activities, with an emphasis upon the growing of crops and periodic communal bison hunts. This religious lore, deposited in the village bundle, was in the hands of a priest who was to manipulate it for the good of the total community. Although the commoners controlled few positions of influence, there were avenues of status achievement open to them in ranked societies accessible through payments and involving participation in warfare and curing. There was a tendency for all of these activities to be brought under religious control. Offensive warfare was never undertaken by the most respected leaders. Women carried on the bulk of the sedentary labor and controlled the use of land and the dwellings.

The Plains horticultural pattern is exemplified by the Caddoan-speaking horticulturalists. Specific divergences from it, or modifications of it, like those of the southern sedentary Siouan speakers, suggest that they came into the area later, or for other reasons made a less successful or less wholehearted adaptation to horticulture. There is evidence of considerable late prehistoric conflict between these native groups which increased tremendously under conditions introduced by the Europeans.

The details of the origin and rise of the nomadic hunting peoples of the Plains and of their culture pattern seem complex and confusing. Much of the complexity may be attributed to the fact that the culture growth of the equestrian nomads did not flow solely out of native factors. In addition, during the period of their ascendancy the nomads came under progressively severe pressures from the encroaching Europeans.

The western Dakota Sioux groups exemplify this new pattern. Their social organization was characterized by a resilience and flexibility in which kinship bonds could be extended to encompass large groups of people without committing them to stable religio-political affiliation. Leadership was a matter of individual initiative and success. In theory, the whole group was equally rewarded by individual achievements. Status mobility was practically unbounded. This individualism was supported by the religion, which allowed for and rewarded personal inventiveness. There were no territorial ties or permanency of residence.

Given the horse, this type of organization became an ideal vehicle for mobile warfare and exploitation of the bison herds. Dependence on the herds alone, however, was insufficient to maintain life, and the equestrian nomads were also dependent on the villages. With their superior strength and mobility, the nomads could be parasitic or symbiotic virtually at will. In other areas of the world at other periods such a conflict has often been resolved by some stable incorporation of these two ways of life, but this did not happen on the Plains; any possibility of aboriginal solutions was prevented by European activities.

As the Europeans advanced their interests and stabilized their bases they were able to utilize native rivalries to further their own aims. With the increase of trade, European industrialization expanded, and at the same time the native peoples became increasingly dependent upon the manufactured goods. In their dwindling villages beset by epidemics and raids, the horticulturalists clung to their old solution of a village way of life and their compromise of nominal friendship with the invading Europeans. They thus became bases of supply and operation for both of their enemies—the nomads and the Europeans.

Even in the face of these severe stresses the horticulturalists did not become horse nomads. It was to the complete disadvantage of those in high places and their supporters to institute a totally nomadic existence. Those elements of the villages, the commoner men, who might be advantaged in becoming nomads were in the least favorable position to voice or to implement their wishes, or to crystallize them into any organized group activity in the face of the weight of tradition and authority. The Caddoan chiefs were able to hold their men in check even though there was a relative increase in the real rewards for parvenu status striving exemplified in the elaboration of various warrior and dancing societies.

The road followed by the nomads took its greatest turn after the weakening of the horticultural villages, the weakening to which they had contributed. The extreme debilitation of the horticulturalists conveniently coincided with the growing disappearance of the buffalo and a rising demand for free land on the part of agricultural groups in the United States. An all-out campaign was waged by the United States Army against the nomads, a long and bitter war intensified by the expanding cattle interests, the extension of railroads, the passage of the Homestead Act, and new population movements.

Aside from Australia, the North American continent was the main area of the world where European colonialism was completely successful. That is to say, European culture was transplanted, and its population took over the territory at the complete expense of the native inhabitants and further developed the pattern of industrialization. This phenomenon was no simple matter of climatic and geographical determinism. More fundamentally, it was a reflection of the level of development of the native cultures in these lands which defined the terms under which they would answer the needs of the Europeans or could meet their threats.

In this chapter of world history it is obvious that indigenous cultural development had reached only the level of socioeconomic advancement which would allow of small autonomous villages or, at best, tribal organization of a rather loose order. This fact was of tremendous significance in determining the steps by which transplanted Old World culture developed on the new continent, and also contributed in characteristic ways to its ascendance.

From the standpoint of general cultural development, the Plains horticulturalists were actually anomalous: they were villagers who had managed with a minimum of surpluses to achieve nascent class stratification, which in such attenuated form is all the more amazing in its tenacity. The contrast between the Caddoan groups and such horticulturalists as the Cheyennes who did become nomads may throw light on the point at which developing societies reach a new level of integration with the emergence of economically stabilized classes. Apparently this level can be reached even with groups possessing limited wealth where, among other things, the wealth is not retained by the upper stratum but simply manipulated by it. The resistance to change among the Caddoan horticulturalists leads one to suspect that once such economically differentiated groups appear with developed religious sanctions, it takes severe social change to remove their traces.

In the absence of fully developed pastoralism on the Plains, the acceptance of nomadism by these people would represent a move away from the security afforded by the horticultural way of life, and, in effect, be a step backward in the level of socio-economic adaptation. Not that such judgments moved the participants. I have tried to show here the motives of the individuals involved: how their own self-interests and the interests of the community would appear to them on the basis of their relative age, their sex, their place in the family, and the status of the family itself—in a word, their position in the general social fabric. The presence of nascent class distinctions with the supporting religion was a primary factor motivating the individual in the struggle to retain the security afforded him by horticulture, with the conviction that this security was a result of those factors. In order to effect significant social change, new developments needed to be of sufficient scope to shake the basis of this fiction.

For all native peoples the final consequences were much alike. Under the weight of European presence native ways went under. Only in marginal regions, in areas difficult of access or unwanted for whatever reason, was survival with any sort of integration possible. In such places much of the old life continues. The people remain, and increasing numbers are planning to stay. We, descendants of the visitor, and the old resident alike, surrounded by a new wilderness of destruction and imbalance, can look back at the earlier ways and the native means with new respect. The history of these people may teach us lessons for the future.

Bibliography of Sources Cited

Benedict, R.

1922   The vision in Plains culture. *American Anthropologist,* n.s. 24:1–23.

1923   The concept of the guardian spirit in North America. Memoir 29, American Anthropological Association. Lancaster, Pa.

Bennett, John W.

1944   The development of ethnological theory as illustrated by studies of the Plains sun dance. *American Anthropologist,* n.s. 46:162–81.

Blair, E. H., trans. and ed.

1911   *The Indian tribes of the upper Mississippi Valley* .... 2 vols. Cleveland: A. H. Clark Co.

Boller, H. A.

1959   *Among the Indians: Eight years in the Far West, 1858–1866,* ed. M. M. Quaife. Chicago: The Lakeside Press.

Bolton, H. E., ed.

1914 *Athanase de Mézières and the Louisiana-Texan frontier, 1768–1780.* 2 vols. Cleveland: A. H. Clark Co.

1916 *Spanish explorations in the Southwest, 1542–1706.* New York: C. Scribner's Sons.

1917 *French intrusions into Mexico, 1749–1752.* In *The Pacific Ocean in history,* ed. H. M. Stephens and H. E. Bolton, pp. 389–407. New York: The Macmillan Co.

Bourne, E. G., ed.

1904 *Narrative of the career of Hernando de Soto.* Trailmaker Series, 2 vols. New York: A. S. Barnes and Co.

Bowers, A. W.

1950 *Mandan social and ceremonial organization.* Chicago: University of Chicago Press.

1965 *Hidatsa social and ceremonial organization.* Bureau of American Ethnology, Bulletin 194. Washington, D.C.: G.P.O.

Bradbury, J.

1904 *Travels in the interior of America in the years 1807, 1810, and 1811.* In *Early Western Travels,* ed. R. G. Thwaites, vol. 5. Cleveland: A. H. Clark Co.

Bruner, E.

1961 *Differential change in the culture of the Mandan from 1250–1953.* In *Perspectives in American Indian culture change,* ed. by Edward H. Spicer. Chicago: University of Chicago Press.

Buckstaff, R. N.

1927 Stars and constellations of a Pawnee sky map. *American Anthropologist,* n.s. 29:279–85.

Carver, J.

1779   *Travels through the interior parts of North America in the years 1766, 1767, and 1768.* Dublin: S. Price.

Casañas de Jesus Maris, Fray F.

1927   Descriptions of the Tejas or Asinai Indians. *Southwestern Historical Quarterly* 30:206–18, 283–304.

Catlin, G.

1967   *O-kee-pa, a religious ceremony and other customs of the Mandans,* ed. J. C. Ewers. New Haven: Yale University Press.

Celiz, F. F.

1935   *Diary of the Alarcon expedition into Texas, 1718–1719,* ed. F. L. Hoffman. Quivira Society Publications, vol. 5. Los Angeles: The Quivira Society.

Chittenden, H. M.

1935   *The American fur trade of the Far West.* 2 vols. New York: The Press of the Pioneers.

Curtis, E. S.

1909   *The North American Indian: The Arikara.* Vol. 5. Cambridge: The University Press.

1930   *The North American Indian: The Wichita.* Vol. 19. Norwood, Mass.: The Plimpton Press.

Dale, H. E., ed.

1941   *The Ashley-Smith explorations and the discovery of a central route to the Pacific, 1822–1829.* Glendale: A. H. Clark Co.

Deetz, J.

1965   *The dynamics of stylistic change in Arikara ceramics.* Urbana: University of Illinois Press.

De Gannes

1934   Memoir of De Gannes concerning the Illinois

Country [attributed to Deliette]. In *The French Foundations, 1680–1693,* ed. T. C. Pease and R. C. Werner. Collections of the Illinois State Historical Library 23:302–95.

Denig, E. T.
1961 *Five Indian tribes of the upper Missouri,* ed. J. C. Ewers. Norman: University of Oklahoma Press.

Dodge, Col. H.
1861 *Report on the expedition of dragoons under Col. Henry Dodge, to the Rocky Mountains in 1835.* House Executive Document 181, 24th Congress, 1st session. Also *American State Papers: Military Affairs* 6:130–46.

Dorsey, G. A.
1902 One of the sacred altars of the Pawnee. Papers of the 13th International Congress of Americanists, pp. 67–74. Easton, Pa.: Eschenbach.

1904a *The mythology of the Wichita.* Carnegie Institution Publication 21. Washington, D.C.: G.P.O.

1904b *Traditions of the Skidi Pawnee.* Memoirs of the American Folk Lore Society, vol. 8. Boston and New York: Houghton and Mifflin Co. for the American Folklore Society.

1904c *Traditions of the Arikara.* Carnegie Institution. Washington, D.C.: G.P.O.

1905 A Pawnee personal medicine shrine. *American Anthropologist,* n.s. 7:496–98.

1906a The Skidi rite of human sacrifice. *Bericht of the 15th International Congress of Americanists,* pt. 2, pp. 65–70. Stuttgart: Kohlhammer.

1906b Social organization of the Skidi Pawnee. *Bericht of the*

15th International Congress of Americanists, pt. 2, pp. 71–77. Stuttgart: Kohlhammer.

1906c Pawnee war tales. *American Anthropologist*, n.s. 8:337–45.

1906d A Pawnee ritual of instruction. In Boas Anniversary Volume, pp. 350–353. New York: J. E. Stechart and Co.

1906e *The Pawnee: Mythology*. Carnegie Institution. Washington, D.C.: G.P.O.

Dorsey, G. A., and Murie, J. R.

1940 Notes on Skidi Pawnee Society. Field Museum of Natural History Anthropological Series, vol. 27, no. 2, pp. 65–119.

Dorsey, J. O.

1894 *Siouan sociology*. 15th Annual Report, Bureau of American Ethnology. Washington, D.C.: G.P.O.

Eggan, F.

1937 The Cheyenne and Arapaho kinship system. In *Social anthropology of North American tribes*, ed. F. Eggan, pp. 35–98. Chicago: University of Chicago Press.

1952 The ethnological cultures and their archeological backgrounds. In *Archeology of the eastern United States*, ed. J. Griffin, pp. 34–45. Chicago: University of Chicago Press.

1955 The Cheyenne and Arapaho kinship system. In *Social anthropology of North American tribes*, ed. F. Eggan, pp. 31–95. Chicago: University of Chicago Press.

1966 *The American Indian: Perspectives for the study of social change*. Chicago: University of Chicago Press.

Ewers, J. C.

1955　*The horse in Blackfoot Indian culture.* Bureau of American Ethnology, Bulletin 159. Washington, D.C.: G.P.O.

Evans, H.

1927　Hugh Evans' journal of Col. Henry Dodge's expedition to the Rocky Mountains in 1835, ed. F. S. Perrine. *Mississippi Valley Historical Review* 14:192–214.

Fletcher, A. C.

1900　Giving thanks: A Pawnee ceremony. *Journal of American Folklore* 13:261–66.

1904　*The Hako: A Pawnee Ceremony.* 22nd Annual Report, Bureau of American Ethnology, part 2. Washington, D.C.: G.P.O.

Fletcher, A. C., and La Flesche, F.

1911　*The Omaha tribe.* 27th Annual Report, Bureau of American Ethnology. Washington, D.C.: G.P.O.

Fortune, R. F.

1932　*Omaha secret societies.* Columbia University Contributions to Anthropology, vol. 14. New York: Columbia University Press.

Frison, George C.

1967　The Piney Creek sites, Wyoming. *University of Wyoming Publications* 33:1–92.

Gates, C. M., ed.

1933　*Five fur traders of the Northwest; being the narrative of Peter Pond . . . .* Minneapolis: University of Minnesota Press.

Gilmore, M. R.

1925a Arikara household shrine to Mother Corn. Museum

of the American Indian, Heye Foundation, *Indian Notes* 2:31–34.

1925b Arikara basketry. Ibid., pp. 89–95.

1926a Arikara commerce. Ibid. 3:13–18.

1926b Arikara genesis and its teachings. Ibid., pp. 188–93.

1927 Notes on Arikara tribal organization. Ibid. 4:332–50.

1928 The making of a new head chief by the Arikara. Ibid. 5:411–18.

1930 The Arikara tribal temple. Ibid. 14:47–70.

1931 The sacred bundles of the Arikara. Ibid. 16:33–50.

Giraud, M.

1945 *Le Métis Canadien: Son rôle dans l'histoire des provinces de l'Ouest.* Travaux et memoires de l'Institute d'Ethnologie, vol. 44. Paris: Presses Universitaires de France.

1953 *Histoire de la Louisiane Française . . . 1698–1715.* Vol. 1. Paris: Presses Universitaires de France.

1958a *Histoire de la Louisiane Française . . . 1715–1717.* Vol. 2. Paris: Presses Universitaires de France.

1958b Etienne Veniard de Bourgmont's "Exact description of Louisiana." *Bulletin of the Missouri Historical Society* 15:3–19.

Grinnell, G. B.

1889 *Pawnee hero stories and folk tales.* New York.

1891a Two Pawnian tribal names. *American Anthropologist* 4:197–99.

1891b Marriage among the Pawnees. Ibid., pp. 275–81.

1892 Development of a Pawnee myth. *Journal of American Folklore* 5:127–34.

1893 Pawnee mythology. Ibid. 6:113–40.

1894 A Pawnee star myth. Ibid. 7:197–200.

1923   *The Cheyenne Indians.* 2 vols. New Haven: Yale University Press.

Haines, F.

1938a Where did the Plains Indians get their horse? *American Anthropologist*, n.s. 40:112–17.

1938b The northward spread of horses among the Plains Indians. *American Anthropologist*, n.s. 40:429–37.

Hamilton, T. M., arranger

1960   Indian trade guns. *Missouri Archaeologist* 22:1–226.

Hammond, G. P., and Rey, A.

1940   *Narratives of the Coronado expeditions, 1540–1542.* University of New Mexico Coronado Cuarto Centennial Publications, vol. 2. Albuquerque: University of New Mexico Press.

Hanson, C. E.

1955   *The northwest gun.* Nebraska Historical Society Publications in Anthropology, no. 2. Lincoln: Nebraska Historical Society.

Hassrick, Royal B.

1944   Teton Dakota kinship system. *American Anthropologist*, n.s. 46:336–47.

Henning, D. R.

1967   Mississippian influences on the eastern Plains border: An evaluation. *Plains Anthropologist*, 12–36, pp. 184–94.

Henry, A.

1921   *Alexander Henry's travels and adventures in the years 1760–1776*, ed. M. M. Quaife. Chicago: The Lakeside Press.

Henry, A., and Thompson, D.

1897   The Manuscript Journals of . . . 1799–1814. In

New light on the early history of the greater North-west, ed. E. Coues. 3 vols. New York: Francis P. Harper.

Hidalgo, F. F.
1927   Description of the Tejas or Asinai Indians, 1691–1722, trans. M. A. Hatcher. *Southwestern Historical Quarterly* 31:50–62.

Hodge, F. W., ed.
1912   *Handbook of the American Indians north of Mexico.* Pt. 2. Bureau of American Ethnology, Bulletin 30. Washington, D.C.: G.P.O.

Hoebel, A.
1960   *The Cheyenne Indians of the Great Plains.* New York: Holt, Rinehart, and Winston.

Holder, P.
1950   Review of *Mandan social and ceremonial organization* by Alfred W. Bowers. *Nebraska History* 30.
1958   Social stratification among the Arikara. *Ethnohistory* 5:210–18.
1968   Review of *An interpretation of Mandan culture history* by W. R. Wood. *American Anthropologist*, n.s. 70:1022–23.
        Field Notes, Arikara.

Houck, L., ed.
1909   *The Spanish regime in Missouri.* 2 vols. Chicago: R. R. Doubleday and Sons Co.

Hunt, G. T.
1940   *The wars of the Iroquois.* Madison: University of Wisconsin Press.

Irving, J. T.
1835   *Indian sketches.* 2 vols. Philadelphia: Cary, Lea, and Blanchard.

Jablow, J.

  1951   *The Cheyenne in Plains Indian trade relations, 1795–
          1840.* American Ethnological Society, Monograph 19.
          New York: J. J. Augustin.

James, E.

  1905   *An account of an expedition from Pittsburgh to the
          Rocky Mountains,* ed. R. G. Thwaites. Early Western
          Travels, vols. 14–17. Cleveland: A. H. Clark Co.

Kellogg, L. P., ed.

  1917   *Early narratives of the Northwest, 1634–1699.* New
          York: C. Scribner's Sons.

  1925   *The French regime in Wisconsin and the Northwest.*
          Madison: Wisconsin State Historical Society.

Kennard, E.

  1936   Mandan grammar. *International Journal of American
          Linguistics* 9:1–43.

Kenton, F., ed.

  1927   *The Indians of North America. Selected and edited
          from the Jesuit Relations and allied documents . . . 1610–
          1791.* 2 vols. New York: Harcourt, Brace and Co.

Kroeber, A. L.

  1939   *Cultural and natural areas of native North America.*
          University of California Publications in American
          Archaeology and Ethnology, vol. 38. Berkeley:
          University of California Press.

La Flesche, F.

  1914   Ceremonies and rituals of the Osage. *Smithsonian
          Miscellaneous Collections,* vol. 62, no. 8, pp. 66–69.

  1921– *The Osage tribe.* 36th, 39th, and 43rd Annual Reports,
    30   Bureau of American Ethnology. Washington, D.C.:
          G.P.O.

Lahontan, A. L. de

1905 *New voyages in western America*, ed. R. G. Thwaites. Chicago: A. C. McClurg and Co. Reprint of the 1703 English ed.; orig. publ. 2 vols., Amsterdam, 1728.

Landes, R.

1968 *The Mystic Lake Sioux*. Madison: University of Wisconsin Press.

Larocque, F. A.

1910 *Journal of . . . from the Assiniboine to the Yellowstone, 1805*. Publications of the Canadian Archives, no. 3. Ottawa: Government Printing Bureau.

La Vérendrye, Le Chevalier de

1927 *Journals and letters of Pierre Gaultier de Varennes de La Vérendrye and his sons*, ed. L. J. Burpee Publications of the Champlain Society. Toronto: The Champlain Society.

Lehmer, D., and Caldwell, W. W.

1966 Trend and traditions in the northern Plains. *American Antiquity* 31:511–16.

Lesser, A.

1930 Levirate and fraternal polyandry among the Pawnee. *Man* 30:98–101.

1933 The Pawnee Ghost Dance hand game. Columbia University Contributions to Anthropology, vol. 16. New York: Columbia University Press.

Lesser, A., and Weltfish, G.

1932 The composition of the Caddoan linguistic stock. *Smithsonian Miscellaneous Collections*, vol. 87, no. 6, pp. 3–15.

Lewis, M., and Clark, W.

1893 *History of the Expedition . . . Lewis and Clark*, ed. E. Coues. 3 vols. New York: Francis P. Harper.

1904– *The original journals of the Lewis and Clark expedition,*
1905 ed. R. G. Thwaites. 8 vols. New York: Dodd, Mead and Co.

Linton, R.

1922 The Thunder ceremony of the Pawnee. Field Museum of Natural History, Department of Anthropology *Leaflet 5*, pp. 1–19.

1923a The sacrifice to the morning star by the Skidi Pawnee. Ibid., *Leaflet 6*, pp. 1–18.

1923b Annual ceremony of the Pawnee medicine men. Ibid., *Leaflet 8*, pp. 1–20.

1926 The origin of the Skidi Pawnee sacrifice to the morning star. *American Anthropologist*, n.s. 28:457–66.

Lounsbury, F. G.

1956 A semantic analysis of Pawnee kinship usage. *Language* 32:158–94.

Lowie, R. H.

1913 Societies of the Hidatsa and Mandan Indians. *Anthropological Papers of the American Museum of Natural History* 11:219–358.

1914 Ceremonialism in North America. *American Anthropologist*, n.s. 16:602–31.

1915 Societies of the Arikara Indians. *Anthropological Papers of the American Museum of Natural History* 11:645–78.

1916 Plains Indian age-societies: Historical and comparative summary. Ibid., pp. 877–984.

1917 Notes on the social organization and customs of the Mandan, Hidatsa, and Crow Indians. Ibid. 21:1–99.

Margry, P.

1876– *Découvertes et établissements . . . dans . . . l'Amérique*
88 *Septentrionale (1614–1754): Mémoires et documents originaux recueillis et publiés par Pierre Margry.* 6 vols. Paris: Maisonneuve et Ch. Leclerc.

Masson, L. R.

1889– *Les Bourgeois de la compagnie du Nord-Ouest.* 2 vols.
90 Quebec: A. Coté et Cie.

Maximilian, Prince of Wied-Neuwied

1906 *Travels in the interior of North America,* ed. R. G. Thwaites. Early Western Travels, vols. 22, 23, and 24. Cleveland: A. H. Clark Co.

Mooney, J.

1896 The Ghost Dance religion and the Sioux outbreak of 1890. 14th Annual Report, Bureau of American Ethnology, pt. 2, pp. 641–1136. Washington, D.C.: G.P.O.

1905– *The Cheyenne Indians.* Memoirs, American Anthro-
1907 pological Association, vol. 1. Lancaster, Pa.

Morfi, F. J.

1935 *History of Texas, 1673–1779,* trans. C. E. Castañeda. Quivira Society Publications, vol. 6. 2 pts. Albuquerque: The Quivira Society.

Morgan, L. H.

1871a Systems of consanguinity and affinity. *Smithsonian Contributions to Knowledge,* vol. 17, Smithsonian Publication No. 218. Washington, D.C.: G.P.O.

1871b The stone and bone implements of the Arickarees. *Annual report of the regents of the University of New York State,* pp. 25–46.

Murie, J. R.

1914   Pawnee Indian societies. *Anthropological Papers of the American Museum of Natural History*, 11: 543–644.

MS(a) The ceremonies of the Pawnee. Arranged and edited by Clark Wissler. Phonetic texts revised and translated by Gene Weltfish. Smithsonian Institution.

MS(b) Skiri Pawnee texts. American Museum of Natural History.

Murray, C. A.

1839   *Travels in North America.* 2 vols. London: R. Bentley.

Nasatir, A. P.

1927   Jacques D'Eglise on the upper Missouri, 1791–1795, and Spanish explorations of the upper Missouri. *Mississippi Valley Historical Review* 14:47–71.

1929– Anglo-Spanish rivalry on the upper Missouri. Ibid.
30   16:359–82, 507–28.

1952   *Before Lewis and Clark: Documents illustrating the history of the Missouri, 1785–1804.* 2 vols. St. Louis: St. Louis Historical Documents Foundation.

Nute, G. L.

1931   *The voyageur.* New York: D. Appleton and Co.

1943   *Caesars of the wilderness.* New York: D. Appleton-Century Co.

Nuttal, T.

1905   *Journal of travels into the Arkansas Territory during the year 1819 . . .,* ed. R. G. Thwaites. Early Western Travels, vol. 13. Cleveland: A. H. Clark Co.

Oliver, S. C.

1962   Ecology and cultural continuity as contributing facts in the social organization of the Plains Indians. *University of California Publications in American Archaeology and Ethnology*, vol. 48, no. 1, pp. 1–90.

Parkman, F.

1947 *The Journals of Francis Parkman*, ed. M. Wade. 2 vols. New York: Harpers.

Parsons, E. C.

1929 Ritual parallels in Pueblo and Plains cultures, with a special reference to the Pawnee. *American Anthropologist*, n.s. 31:642–54.

Paul Wilhelm, Duke of Wurtemberg

1941 First journey to North America. *South Dakota Historical Collections* 19 (1938):469–72.

Perrin du Lac, M.

1807 *Travels through the two Louisianas in 1801, 1802, and 1803.* London: R. Phillips for J. G. Barnard.

Pike, Z. M.

1895 *The Expeditions of Zebulon Montgomery Pike . . . 1805, 1806, 1807*, ed. E. Coues. 3 vols. New York: F. P. Harper.

Platt, Mrs. E. G.

1918 Some experiences as a teacher among the Pawnees. *Collections of Kansas State Historical Society* 14:784–94.

Pond, P.

1933 The narrative of Peter Pond. In *Five fur traders of the Northwest*, ed. C. M. Gates, pp. 11–59. Minneapolis: University of Minnesota Press.

Roe, F. G.

1951 *The North American buffalo.* Toronto: University of Toronto Press.

1955   *The Indian and the horse.* Norman: University of Oklahoma Press.

Russell, C. P.

1962   *Guns on the early frontiers: A history of firearms from colonial times through the years of the western fur trade.* Berkeley: University of California Press.

1967   *Firearms, traps, and tools of the mountain men.* New York: Alfred Knopf.

Sapir, E.

1916   *Time perspective in aboriginal American culture.* Canadian Geological Survey, Memoir 90. Anthropological Series, no. 13. pp. 1–87. Ottawa: Government Printing Bureau.

Schoolcraft, H. R.

1851   *Personal memoirs of a residence of thirty years with the Indian tribes on the American frontiers, A.D. 1812–1842.* Philadelphia: Lippincott, Grambo & Co.

1851–   *Historical and statistical information, respecting the*
57   *history, condition and prospects of the Indian tribes of the United States.* Vols. 5 and 6. Philadelphia: Lippincott Co.

Secoy, F. R.

1953   *Changing military patterns on the Great Plains.* American Ethnological Society, Monograph 21. Locust Valley, N.J.: J. J. Augustin.

Solis, F. G. J. de

1931   Diary of a visit of inspection of the Texas missions . . . 1767–1768, trans. M. K. Kress. *Southwestern Historical Quarterly* 35:28–76.

Spier, L.

1921   The sun dance of the Plains Indians: Its development and diffusion. *Anthropological Papers of the American Museum of Natural History* 16, no. 7, pp. 451–527.

Stands in Timber, J., and Liberty, M.

1967   *Cheyenne memories.* New Haven: Yale University Press.

Strong, W. D.

1933   The Plains Culture Area in the light of archeology. *American Anthropologist*, n.s. 35:271–87.

1935   An Introduction to Nebraska archeology. *Smithsonian Miscellaneous Collections*, vol. 93, no. 10, pp. 1–323.

1936   Anthropological theory and archeological fact. In *Essays in anthropology presented to A. L. Kroeber*, ed. R. H. Lowie, pp. 359–70. Berkeley: University of California Press.

1940   From history to prehistory in the northern Great Plains. *Smithsonian Miscellaneous Collections* 100:353–94.

Swanton, J. R.

1911   *Indian tribes of the lower Mississippi Valley.* Bureau of American Ethnology, Bulletin 43. Washington, D.C.: G.P.O.

1930   Some neglected data bearing on Cheyenne, Chippewa, and Dakota history. *American Anthropologist*, n.s. 32:156–60.

1939   The survival of horses brought to North America by De Soto. *American Anthropologist*, n.s. 41:170–71.

1942   *Source material on the history and ethnology of the Caddo Indians.* Bureau of American Ethnology, Bulletin 132. Washington, D.C.: G.P.O.

Tabeau, P. A.

1939 *Tabeau's narrative of Loisel's expedition to the upper Missouri,* ed. A. H. Abel. Norman: University of Oklahoma Press.

Thomas, A. B.

1935 *After Coronado: Spanish exploration northeast of New Mexico, 1696–1727.* Norman: University of Oklahoma Press.

1940 *The Plains Indians and New Mexico, 1751–1778 . . . .* Albuquerque: University of New Mexico Press.

Thompson, D.

1962 *David Thompson's narrative of his explorations in western America, 1784–1812,* ed. J. B. Tyrell. Publications of the Champlain Society, vol. 12. Toronto: The Champlain Society.

Tixier, V.

1940 *Tixier's travels on the Osage prairies,* ed. J. F. McDermott, trans. A. J. Salvan. Norman: University of Oklahoma Press.

Trudeau, J. B.

1914 Journal of Jean Baptiste Trudeau. *South Dakota Historical Collections* 7:403–74.

Twitchell, R. E.

1914 *The Spanish archives of New Mexico.* 2 vols. Cedar Rapids: The Torch Press.

Voegelin, C. F.

1941 Internal relationships of Siouan languages. *American Anthropologist,* n.s. 42:246–49.

Voegelin, C. F., and Voegelin, F. M.

1964 Languages of the world. *Anthropological Linguistics,* vol. 6, no. 6, pp. 79–134.

Waring, A. J., Jr., and Holder, P.
1945 A prehistoric ceremonial complex in the southeastern United States. *American Anthropologist*, n.s. 47:1–34.

Webb, W. P.
1931 *The Great Plains: A study in institutions and environment.* Boston: Ginn and Co.

Wedel, W. R.
1936 *An introduction to Pawnee archeology.* Bureau of American Ethnology, Bulletin 112. Washington, D.C.: G.P.O.

1938 The direct-historical approach to Pawnee archeology. *Smithsonian Miscellaneous Collections*, vol. 97, no. 7. pp. 1–21.

1959 *An introduction to Kansas archeology.* Bureau of American Ethnology, Bulletin 172. Washington, D.C.: G.P.O.

1961 *Prehistoric man on the Great Plains.* Norman: University of Oklahoma Press.

Weltfish, G.
1936 The vision story of Fox boy. *International Journal of American Linguistics* 9:44–76.

1937 *Caddoan texts: Pawnee, South Band dialect.* Publications of the American Ethnological Society, vol. 17. New York: G. E. Stechart.

1965 *The lost universe.* New York: Basic Books, Inc.

Will, G. F.
1924 Archeology of the Missouri Valley. *Anthropological Papers of the American Museum of Natural History* 20, pt. 6, pp. 285–344.

Will, G. F., and Hecker, T. C.

1944 The upper Missouri aboriginal culture in North Dakota. *North Dakota Historical Quarterly* 11:5–134.

Will, G. F., and Spinden, H. J.

1906 The Mandans. Peabody Museum Papers, vol. 3, no. 4, pp. 81–219.

Willey, G. R.

1966 *An introduction to American archaeology*. North and Middle America, vol. 1. Englewood Cliffs: Prentice-Hall, Inc.

Winship, G. P.

1896 The Coronado expedition, 1540–1542. 14th Annual Report, Bureau of American Ethnology, pt. 1, pp. 329–613. Washington, D.C.: G.P.O.

Wissler, C.

1906 Diffusion of culture in the Plains. *Bericht of the 15th International Congress of Americanists*, pt. 2, pp. 39–52. Stuttgart: Kohlhammer.

1914 The influence of the horse in the development of Plains culture. *American Anthropologist*, n.s. 16:1–25.

1915 Comparative study of Pawnee and Blackfoot rituals. *Proceedings of the 19th International Congress of Americanists*, pp. 335–39. Washington.

1917 *The American Indian*. New York: Oxford University Press.

1920 The sacred bundles of the Pawnee. *Natural History* 20:569–71.

Wissler, C., and Spinden, H. J.

1916 The Pawnee human sacrifice to the morning star. *American Museum Journal* 16:49–55.

Wolff, H.

    1950   Comparative Siouan I. *International Journal of American Linguistics* 16:61–66.

Wood, W. R.

    1967   *An interpretation of Mandan culture history.* River Basins Surveys Papers, no. 39, Bureau of American Ethnology. Washington, D.C.: G.P.O.

Index

Adaptation. *See* Culture change

Adena archeological complex, 38

Aguayo (Spanish explorer), 13

Aksarben Aspect, 24–27

Alarçon, Martin de, 13

American Fur Company, 19

Animal lodges: Arikara, 48–52 passim; Dakota Sioux, 127; Mandan, 72; Omaha, 77. *See also* Doctors

Anthropologists, glorification of nomads, 110–11

Arikara (language), 33

Arikaras: location, ix, 27, 33–34, 100, 131–33; nomadism, 104–5; population, 71, 85, 118; relations with other groups, 34–35, 78, 91, 104, 126; religion, 42–44, 47, 49–50, 128; social structure, 53–56, 57 n 28, 60, 72, 81, 129; trade, 79, 97, 119, 120, 123

Assiniboins, 32

Astronomy, 44, 76

Barrios y Juarequi, Jacinto de, 14

Barter, 119. *See also* Trade

Beauharnois, 12

Benedict, Ruth, x, 57 n 28, 127–28

Bienville, Jean Baptiste le Moyne de, 10

Bison, 112–13, 118; hunt, 115, 118; ceremonies, 47, 71, 135

Blackbird (Omaha chief), 77, 82

Blackfeet, 99, 100

Bonilla, Francisco Leya de, 5

Bourgmont, Etienne Véniard de, 8, 10, 11, 111

Bow, use of, 115

Bowers, A. W., 72–73

Boys, 53–56, 108–9, 129, 133–34

Bradbury, J., 124

169